East Africa 1917–18

King's African Rifles Soldier

COMBAT

VERSUS

Schutztruppe Soldier

Gregg Adams

First published in Great Britain in 2016 by Osprey Publishing,
PO Box 883, Oxford, OX1 9PL, UK
1385 Broadway, 5th Floor, New York, NY 10018, USA
E-mail: info@ospreypublishing.com

Osprey Publishing, part of Bloomsbury Publishing Plc

A CIP catalogue record for this book is available from the British Library

Print ISBN: 978 1 4728 1327 5
PDF ebook ISBN: 978 1 4728 1328 2
ePub ebook ISBN: 978 1 4728 1329 9

Index by Rob Munro
Typeset in Univers, Sabon and Adobe Garamond Pro
Maps by bounford.cpm
Originated by PDQ Media, Bungay, UK
Printed in China through World Print Ltd.

16 17 18 19 20   10 9 8 7 6 5 4 3 2 1

Osprey Publishing supports the Woodland Trust, the UK's leading
woodland conservation charity. Between 2014 and 2018 our donations
are being spent on their Centenary Woods project in the UK.

www.ospreypublishing.com

Acknowledgements

The author wishes to thank the copying staff of The National Archives
(UK) for their quick response to orders for copies of records used in
researching this book. Thanks are also due to the Interlibrary Loan Staff
of the Prince William County Virginia Public Library (USA) for their
support in locating and securing loans of research materials.

Author's note

In this book the term 'British' is used to denote British Empire forces,
including Indians, European South Africans and Africans. Similarly,
'German' indicates European and African forces under German command.

Imperial War Museums Collections

Many of the photos in this book come from the huge collections of
IWM (Imperial War Museums) which cover all aspects of conflict
involving Britain and the Commonwealth since the start of the twentieth
century. These rich resources are available online to search, browse and
buy at www.iwmcollections.org.uk. In addition to Collections Online,
you can visit the Visitor Rooms where you can explore over 8 million
photographs, thousands of hours of moving images, the largest sound
archive of its kind in the world, thousands of diaries and letters written
by people in wartime, and a huge reference library. To make an
appointment, call (020) 7416 5320, or e-mail mail@iwm.org.uk
Imperial War Museums www.iwm.org.uk

Comparative officer ranks

British	German
Field Marshal[1]	*Generalfeldmarschall*[2]
General[1]	*Generaloberst*[2]
Lieutenant-General (Lt-Gen)	*General der Infanterie/Kavallerie*[2]
Major-General (Maj-Gen)	*Generalleutnant*[2]
Brigadier-General (Brig-Gen)	*Generalmajor*
Colonel (Col)	*Oberst*
Lieutenant-Colonel (Lt-Col)	*Oberstleutnant*
Major (Maj)	*Major*
Captain (Capt)	*Hauptmann*
Lieutenant (Lt)	*Oberleutnant*
Second Lieutenant (2/Lt)	*Leutnant*

1. No British officers held these ranks in East Africa.
2. No German officers held these ranks in East Africa.

Key to military symbols

Army Group	Army	Corps	Division	Brigade	Regiment	Battalion
Company/Battery	Platoon	Section	Squad	Infantry	Artillery	Cavalry
Airborne	Unit HQ	Air defence	Air Force	Air mobile	Air transportable	Amphibious
Anti-tank	Armour	Air aviation	Bridging	Engineer	Headquarters	Maintenance
Medical	Missile	Mountain	Navy	Nuclear, biological, chemical	Ordnance	Parachute
Reconnaissance	Signal	Supply	Transport movement	Fortress or static	Fortress machine gun	

Key to unit identification

Unit identifier / Parent unit / Commander
(+) with added elements
(−) less elements

CONTENTS

Introduction

During World War I the tangled bush country of British, German and Portuguese colonies in East Africa became a battleground for Germany and Britain. By 1917 and 1918 this campaign was fought by two colonial armies of indigenous East African soldiers (askaris) led by whites: the Kaiserlichen Schutztruppe für Deutsche-Ostafrika (Imperial Protectorate Force for German East Africa) and the British King's African Rifles (KAR). Both originated in the years before World War I and were intended to subdue indigenous resistance and maintain order in the newly established British and German colonies. In German East Africa – now mainland Tanzania, Rwanda and Burundi – the Schutztruppe was formed; in the British colonies – the British East Africa Protectorate (today's Kenya); Nyasaland (today's Malawi);

Schutztruppe askaris are led by musicians during a parade in Dar es Salaam, German East Africa, in 1914. This photograph reflects the image that Germans sought to cultivate of indigenous peoples loyal to the Kaiser and Imperial Germany. In reality, askari loyalty was based on traditional African values of small-group fellowship and personal attachment to immediate leaders. These factors were augmented by high pay (at least before 1914) and being granted extraordinary privileges compared to the rest of the local population. (Photo by Hulton Archive/ Getty Images)

and Uganda – the King's African Rifles was created. Pre-war planning did not envisage these forces fighting one another, primarily because both colonial governments feared that a large indigenous army could rebel during or after a war.

When war came to East Africa, the Schutztruppe commander, Oberstleutnant Paul Emil von Lettow-Vorbeck, determined how it was fought. He decided that the best use of his force was to tie down as many British soldiers for as long as possible to keep them from Europe where victory and defeat would be decided. Therefore, he planned to conduct an aggressive defence of German East Africa and, to provide the needed force, started to increase the Schutztruppe in size and strength at the outbreak of war. The Schutztruppe grew to seven times its pre-war size by March 1916, when its strength peaked.

The Imperial German Navy's cruiser SMS *Königsberg* was at Dar es Salaam upon the outbreak of war and promptly began operations aimed at disrupting British seaborne commerce. The British Admiralty was determined not to allow colonial ports to remain in German hands; nor would it allow the Imperial German Navy's long-range radio system, using overseas relay stations, to remain operable: the threat to Britain's merchant shipping was considered too great. To deny bases to German raiders, British ground and amphibious operations were launched against all German colonies. Additionally, capturing German colonies would either expand the British Empire, or provide useful bargaining chips at a peace conference after the war.

During November 1914 British troops from India attacked the port of Tanga, on the Indian Ocean, in north-eastern German East Africa. This attack failed and the British re-embarked during night time, abandoning eight serviceable machine guns, 455 rifles and over 500,000 rounds of ammunition. This was a clear German victory that boosted the morale of the Schutztruppe and German colonists and seemed to justify Lettow-Vorbeck's strategy. Between December 1914 and March 1916, British strategy in East Africa was limited to defending Britain's colonies.

A British offensive to conquer German East Africa began in March 1916 with a force that included over 20,000 South African volunteers. Lt-Gen Jan Christiaan Smuts, a former Boer, commanded the British effort. Smuts' offensive drove the Germans from the border of Kenya to the Rufigi River and out of the western area of German East Africa. His supply system broke down,

British soldiers in East Africa in 1916. In the centre, a soldier of 2nd Kashmir Rifles, a unit of the Indian Imperial Service Force, is flanked by two askaris of the 4th King's African Rifles that was recruited in Uganda. To the British at home, this image would have represented the extent of their Empire by illustrating the diversity of peoples loyally serving the King-Emperor. During 1914 and 1915, troops from India provided the majority of British infantry in East Africa, while little was done to recruit askaris and expand the King's African Rifles. (Photo by Culture Club/Getty Images)

The British Empire's command team from May 1917: Lt-Gen Jacob Louis van Deventer (right) and his chief of staff, Brig-Gen Seymour Hulbert Sheppard (left). Van Deventer was a South African and one of the few Boer professional soldiers of the old Transvaal State Artillery. He commanded a South African division during Lt-Gen Jan Christiaan Smuts' 1916 campaign and learned the lessons of fighting in East Africa. He personally chose Sheppard, a British regular and veteran East African brigade commander, as his chief of staff. Together they were a capable command team that led the British until the end of the war. (© IWM Q 15403)

however, and a consequent lack of supplies and the spread of disease reduced his force to skeleton strength. Smuts proclaimed victory and left East Africa when the rainy season halted operations in January 1917; but his proclamation was seen to be premature when Lettow-Vorbeck decided the war was not over and continued the fight, employing his strategy of a mobile defence.

Maj-Gen Reginald Hoskins replaced Smuts in command. Hoskins, formerly Inspector-General of the King's African Rifles, reorganized the supply system, accelerated expansion of the regiment and prepared the British forces for a new campaign. He was not to lead the next offensive, however. On 29 May 1917, another South African and former Boer leader, Lt-Gen Jacob Louis van Deventer, took command of the British forces in East Africa with orders to attack the Germans and end the campaign. Using troops landed at Kilwa and Lindi (ports in south-eastern German East Africa) and forces from the west, he launched concentric attacks against the Schutztruppe. Van Deventer's dispatch (dated 21 January 1918) provides an insight into his thinking. After explaining why there were no geographical objectives to conquer, he stated: 'It therefore became obvious to me that our true objectives in the coming campaign must be the enemy forces in the field, and that the

The commander of the Schutztruppe in August 1914, Oberstleutnant Paul von Lettow-Vorbeck, became a legend as a result of his leadership during the four years of war. He had served in China during the Boxer Rebellion and in German South West Africa during the Herero and Hottentot rebellion. Recent scholarship in Germany has diminished the reputation he earned during and after World War I; some contend that his post-war reputation was built up by his British opponents to justify their failures. It is undeniable, however, that he held the core of the Schutztruppe together in trying circumstances until the war ended. (Photo by Keystone/Hulton Archive/Getty Images)

completion of the conquest of German East Africa could only be brought about by hard hitting, and plenty of it' (Supplement to *The London Gazette*, 5 April 1918).

Lettow-Vorbeck's objectives for the 1917 dry season (May to November) were simple: to survive until the rains forced an end to operations, which would force the British into another year of campaigning in a strategically insignificant theatre. He had no intention of defending territory for its own sake; ground was only important insofar as it produced food supplies. Inland from Lindi was one such area which Lettow-Vorbeck described as 'very fertile and known as the granary of the colony', and which he noted was 'in a very precarious position, and it was necessary to consider what should be done if it were lost' (Lettow-Vorbeck (n.d.): 190). He planned to continue his mobile delaying campaign and keep the British from crop-growing areas until the 1917 harvest was collected in August and September. He also intended to exploit any mistakes arising from the British order to inflict tactical defeats through local attacks. With King's African Rifles battalions providing over half of van Deventer's infantry strength, the stage was set for a contest between the askaris of the Schutztruppe and the King's African Rifles.

MAP KEY

1 2–5 November 1914: An amphibious attack by a British force from India is defeated by the Schutztruppe at Tanga in German East Africa. This victory appears to vindicate Lettow-Vorbeck's strategy for the war in German East Africa; it gives him the status of a victorious commander, and raises the Schutztruppe's morale.

2 1915: Schutztruppe raiding parties attack the Uganda Railway throughout the year. While actual damage is minimal, these raids feed the British colony's fear of a German invasion and result in more British forces being sent to East Africa.

3 22 June 1915: British forces attack across Lake Victoria and capture Bukoba to destroy the long-range radio station there. They then return to British territory. This raiding force includes troops of 4th Battalion, KAR and demonstrates their battle skills.

4 July 1915: The last member of the Imperial German Navy's overseas fleet, the pre-war cruiser, SMS *Königsberg*, is destroyed in the Rufigi River delta by the Royal Navy, removing its threat to British merchant shipping in the Indian Ocean.

5 5 March 1916: British forces (over half from the Union of South Africa) invade German East Africa from British East Africa. These are shortly joined by Belgian forces (indigenous troops with European leaders) advancing from the north-west and British forces from Northern Rhodesia and Nyasaland that were composed of white South Africans and indigenous personnel from both the King's African Rifles and police.

6 January 1917: Major British offensive operations come to a halt as the rainy season results in massive flooding of the rivers' bottom lands; the British supply system collapses as a result of the atrocious weather and fly-borne diseases that kill the draught animals that are used to move supplies forward.

7 September 1916: British forces land at the Indian Ocean ports of Kilwa and Lindi and establish bases for the next offensive while eliminating possible unloading locations for any blockade-runners from Germany.

8 May–June 1917: British and Belgian forces launch a renewed offensive. Concentric columns attempt to close on the Schutztruppe to force a stand-up battle which the British hope will end the campaign.

9 18 August 1917: At the battle of Narunyu, a King's African Rifles battalion attempts to outflank and entrap a German force. Hard fighting ensues when the Germans counter-attack, hoping to destroy the flanking British unit. Instead, the King's African Rifles stop the determined Schutztruppe effort, and show that they are on the path to becoming the Schutztruppe's equals.

10 16–18 October 1917: In the largest action of the war in East Africa, the battle of Nyangao–Mahiwa, both sides fight to a standstill while suffering heavy casualties. The German commander reduces his force, leaves behind the wounded, sick and fainthearted and moves into Portuguese East Africa to conduct a large-scale raid.

11 May–November 1917: The Schutztruppe's Westtruppen conducts a fighting withdrawal in an effort to link up with Lettow–Vorbeck's main force in the south-east portion of German East Africa. Pressed by British and Belgian forces, the Germans slowly retreat to the south-east.

12 28 November 1917: The Westtruppen finds British troops in its front and rear. Having been without word of Lettow-Vorbeck's location, the force surrenders. This reduces the surviving Schutztruppe by nearly a half.

13 December 1917–July 1918: The surviving Schutztruppe march across Portuguese East Africa, frequently defeating Portuguese and collecting captured supplies, weapons and ammunition.

14 30–31 August 1918: In the battle of Lioma the Schutztruppe attacks a King's African Rifles position, intent on overrunning it and capturing supplies. Instead, a King's African Rifles battalion stops the Schutztruppe and holds its position on 30 August. The next day, the German force is nearly caught in between the three battalions of a King's African Rifles column and makes a narrow escape, losing a field hospital and considerable supplies in the process.

15 25 November 1918: The Schutztruppe surrenders to British forces at Abercorn in Northern Rhodesia after having learned that the war has ended in Europe.

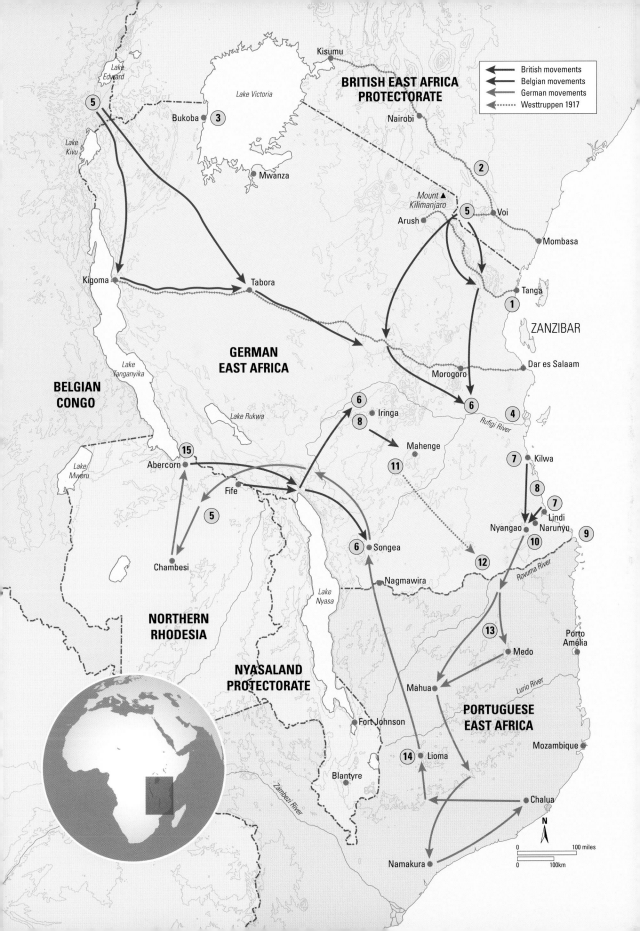

Lake Edward

⑤

Lake Kivu

Lake Tanganyika

BELGIAN CONGO

Lake Mweru

Kigoma

Bukoba ③

Lake Victoria

Mwanza

Kisumu

BRITISH EAST AFRICA PROTECTORATE

Nairobi

②

Mount ▲ *Kilimanjaro*

Arush

⑤

Voi

Mombasa

Tanga

①

ZANZIBAR

	British movements
	Belgian movements
	German movements
	Westtruppen 1917

Tabora

GERMAN EAST AFRICA

Morogoro

⑥

④

Dar es Salaam

Lake Rukwa

⑥ Iringa

⑧

Mahenge

⑪

Rufigi River

⑦ Kilwa

⑧

⑦ Lindi

Narunyu

⑮

Abercorn

Fife

⑤

Chambesi

⑥ Songea

Nagmawira

Lake Nyasa

Nyangao

⑩

⑨

⑫

Rovuma River

NORTHERN RHODESIA

NYASALAND PROTECTORATE

Fort Johnson

Blantyre

Zambezi River

⑬

Medo

Porto Amélia

Mahua

Lurio River

PORTUGUESE EAST AFRICA

Mozambique

⑭ Lioma

Chalua

Namakura

N

0 ——— 100 miles

0 ——— 100km

The Opposing Sides

ORIGINS AND WARTIME EXPANSION

King's African Rifles

In August 1914 the manpower of the King's African Rifles was comprised of 70 British officers (BOs), three British non-commissioned officers (BNCOs) and 2,325 Africans. 1st Battalion, KAR, recruited in Nyasaland, had its HQ and four companies stationed there; its other four companies were in Kenya. 3rd Battalion, KAR, recruited and stationed in Kenya, consisted of five infantry companies and one camel company. 4th Battalion, KAR, recruited and stationed in Uganda, consisted of seven companies. Each of these 21 companies was equipped with one machine gun. The King's African Rifles did not possess artillery, nor were there any British artillery units in the British East African territories.

Britain's military leaders decided not to expand the King's African Rifles at the start of the war. This decision was based on several reasons: the lack of a coherent strategy regarding the role of British East African territories in the event of a war with Germany; the prevailing idea that the war would be of short duration; a traditional reliance upon the Indian Army to provide troops for operations in regions such as East Africa; and the fear of arming Africans who might revolt given the opportunity presented by a war between the European colonial powers. In November 1914 the British decided to defend East Africa using troops from India, and by year's end 10½ battalions from India were in Kenya and Uganda.

In January 1915, the British commander in Kenya, Maj-Gen Richard Wapshare, proposed an expansion of the King's African Rifles to the War Office and requested authorization to raise two new battalions. The Colonial Office and Governor in Nairobi, the Kenyan capital, opposed expansion. The Governor reported that only 600 suitable recruits could be obtained to replace losses in

existing King's African Rifles units; and because the King's African Rifles was controlled by the Colonial Office, only this limited increase in strength was approved in February 1915. A War Office commission, led by Colonel Henry Kitchener – brother of Lord Kitchener, the Secretary of State for War – went to East Africa to investigate the local manpower situation. The commission's report opposed expansion of the King's African Rifles; but Lord Cranworth, a commission member and an expert on East Africa, strongly dissented, stating that 'the main line to be pursued must lie in the most rapid expansion possible of the existing King's African Rifles' (quoted in Holdern 1990: 133 fn2).

Defensive operations during 1915 showed the askari to be a solid soldier and the right one for fighting in this theatre, and confirmed the debilitating effects of the East African climate on the health of non-African troops. One European infantry battalion was reduced from 750 effectives to 265 between 8 March and 19 June 1915. Indian units were reporting sick lists of 20 per cent of their strength. Only African troops were maintaining their strength in the field.

The need for African manpower was finally recognized. At the end of 1915, 500 recruits were requested from Nyasaland; a call that in fact yielded 984 recruits and 180 returned veterans. In April 1916, 2nd Battalion, KAR was re-formed in Nairobi using these men. Shortly after becoming the British commander in East Africa, Smuts had requested that three more King's

African Rifles battalions be raised. Soon, 2nd, 3rd and 4th battalions, KAR were each expanded into regiments of two battalions each. Detachments of 3rd Battalion, KAR in northern Kenya were transferred into a new 5th King's African Rifles. By June 1916 the King's African Rifles comprised five regiments; 1st and 5th King's African Rifles each had one field battalion and a depot; 2nd, 3rd and 4th King's African Rifles each had two field battalions and a depot. Expansion continued, with a third battalion added to 2nd, 3rd and 4th King's African Rifles between October 1916 and June 1917, while 1st King's African Rifles was organized into three field battalions and a depot. In February 1917, two new King's African Rifles regiments were formed: 6th King's African Rifles of two battalions, recruited in the areas of Tanganyika from which the Germans had been driven out, and including captured Schutztruppe askaris recruited from POW camps; and 7th King's African Rifles, one battalion strong and formed in Zanzibar. In 1918, fourth battalions were added to 1st, 2nd and 3rd King's African Rifles, while 4th King's African Rifles was expanded to six battalions to take advantage of Uganda's greater manpower resources. At the war's end the King's African Rifles consisted of 22 battalions in seven regiments: 1st, 2nd, and 3rd King's African Rifles, each of four battalions; 4th King's African Rifles, of six battalions; 5th King's African Rifles, of one battalion; 6th King's African Rifles, of two battalions; and 7th King's African Rifles, of one battalion.

Schutztruppe

By August 1914, the Schutztruppe comprised 68 German combat officers, 60 German warrant officers and NCOs, 132 German medical and non-combatant officers, 184 African NCOs and 2,286 askaris. Roughly two-thirds of the askaris were recruited in German East Africa and the remaining one-third were from Sudan, Ethiopia and Somalia. These officers, NCOs and askaris formed 14 independent *Feldkompagnien* (FKs) numbered 1. FK to 14. FK. The 14 companies were deployed across the colony, with internal security being their primary mission prior to August 1914. German East Africa's paramilitary police numbered 55 Europeans and 2,160 askaris, many of whom were Schutztruppe veterans. Another 1,670 Europeans in German East Africa were registered reservists. The number of Europeans was increased by personnel from the Imperial German Navy (including the officers and crew of the cruiser *Königsberg* in 1915) and from German merchant ships trapped in the colony's ports by the Royal Navy blockade.

An expansion of the Schutztruppe commenced upon the outbreak of war. In August 1914, reserve askaris and new recruits were organized into four new companies numbered 15. FK to 18. FK. Additional companies were formed during the remainder of 1914 and 1915. Two new companies were designated 'reserve', eight were given letters, and several were named. German reservists, some of whom were former Schutztruppe officers and NCOs, were formed into European *Schützenkompagnien* (SchKs) on the outbreak of war, two of which, 7. SchK and 8. SchK, were mounted infantry for use on the border between German East Africa and Kenya. Naval and merchant marine personnel were employed in technical specialist roles, coastal defence, artillery (especially the crews of the 4.1in main battery guns from *Königsberg* which were converted to heavy artillery), and in one company-sized unit named for *Königsberg* (subsequently broken up and its personnel dispersed). European units were reorganized to make better use of skilled European personnel as leader cadres; several *Schützenkompagnien* were reorganized as *Feldkompagnien* while retaining their designations, and others disbanded. In March 1916 the Schutztruppe reached its peak size and strength with 60 company-sized units, headquarters, and support detachments consisting of 3,007 Europeans and 12,100 Africans.

The Schutztruppe originated in 1888 after an African uprising drove the German East Africa Company out of most of Tanganyika. The Imperial Government duly took over the East Africa Company's territory and created a special military force to conquer Tanganyika. Soldiers for the Schutztruppe were initially recruited from Sudanese troops rendered surplus from the Khedival Egyptian Army following the British occupation of Egypt. Initially there were six 100-man companies of Sudanese; another 100-man company was recruited from Portuguese East Africa and referred to as 'Zulus'. In 1891 the Schutztruppe was taken into Imperial service. Personnel and administration were under the auspices of the Imperial German Navy, while finances and operations were under the Colonial Section of the Foreign Ministry. Pictured in the days before the war, this Schutztruppe *Feldkompagnie* is ordered with its three platoons in column and its two Maxim machine guns set up on its right flank. The uniforms are clean, and may well have been freshly issued for the parade. By 1917 and 1918, looking this polished was only a memory. Internal security of the colony was the primary role envisaged by most colonial officials before August 1914, and this image of an ordered unit goes part way to explain the Schutztruppe's ability to awe many potential indigenous adversaries. (© BArch, Bild 105-DOA6612 / Walther Dobbertin)

This plate shows an askari private ejecting a spent cartridge from his rifle during a battle against the Schutztruppe near Lioma, Portuguese East Africa, in late August 1918. He and his comrades have been in the field, marching almost daily in pursuit of the remaining German force under Lettow-Vorbeck's command. While his uniform and boots are worn and stained, his weapons are kept clean and serviceable.

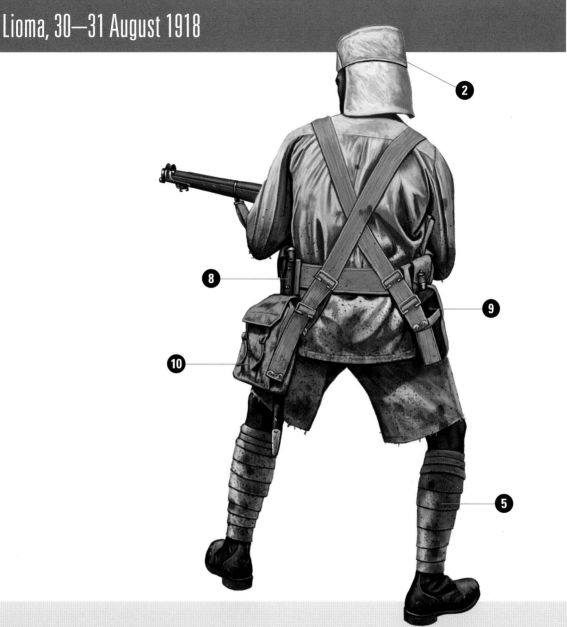

Weapons, dress and equipment

By 1918 the King's African Rifles was uniformly equipped with the .303in Short Magazine Lee Enfield rifle (**1**), the standard British rifle of the war. Because of the confining space in which to manoeuvre one's rifle, the 17in-long bayonet was only fitted just before a bayonet charge.

This askari wears the regulation pillbox field cap (**2**) with a cloth cover to protect the back of the neck. Both the cap and the cover cloth are coloured a pale shade of khaki. The lightweight uniform tunic (**3**) he wears is the Tropical Khaki Battle Dress tunic. Instead of trousers, the askari is wearing the Tropical Khaki Bermuda-style shorts (**4**) which were made from the same material as the tunic. These were also called Khaki Drill (KD). KD was designed for use in warmer climates and was made from a lighter-weight cloth in a paler shade than that used in cooler climates such as France.

This askari is wearing khaki-coloured puttees (**5**) and brown leather ammunition boots (**6**). He is also wearing the standard British Army 1908 webbing equipment in 'battle order', which means that he is not carrying a back pack. The belt is 3in wide and the straps are 2in wide. The following pieces of the webbing are worn: two cartridge pack sets (**7**), one on the right side and one on the left, with each set having five pouches and each pouch containing three five-round clips, providing 150 rounds in total; a Pattern 07 sword bayonet (**8**) in the 'frog' – a tubular carrier connected to the webbing belt; one water bottle (**9**) in its carrier; a haversack (**10**): a rectangular bag approximately 11×9×2in and with a cover secured by two small straps and buckles. Since the askaris did not carry British iron rations due to dietary differences, this kit, including weapon and ammunition, weighed in at about 44lb.

ORGANIZATION, WEAPONS AND TACTICS

King's African Rifles

In 1917, the lightweight Lewis gun was added to the King's African Rifles' arsenal. The .303in Lewis gun weighed 28lb, was equipped with a bipod mount, and used a top-mounted 47-round drum magazine. Its nominal rate of fire was 550rds/min, but this was not practical in combat conditions. The key to the Lewis gun's light weight was that rather than being water cooled it was air cooled. The steel barrel had heat-conducting fins made of aluminium, which conducts heat more efficiently than steel, attached to it. The distinctive 'tube' look of the gun was created by a metal shroud that enclosed the fins. The Lewis gun was originally conceived as a light machine gun that could be produced quicker and more cheaply than the Vickers Mk I heavy machine gun. It could be carried by one man, fired from the hip, and taken places where the Vickers could not. Infantry officers quickly grasped the concept that the Lewis was an integral piece of the infantry company's, and later infantry platoon's, weaponry. The Lewis gun revolutionized infantry tactics and led to the proliferation of such weapons until they became, and remain to this day, integral to the infantry squad/section. (© IWM FIR 9220)

At the start of the war, the King's African Rifles were the only British troops in East Africa who were experienced in bush warfare. In their internal-security role, they frequently conducted expeditions against tribes in East Africa. This work sensitized all ranks to fighting in the bush where sections frequently operated independently and utilized individual fire. Given the dispersal of King's African Rifles companies in scattered stations, battalion-level training was not feasible; nor were funds for such training budgeted by the Colonial Office. As a result, King's African Rifles companies found themselves scattered among larger British forces to serve as advance and flank detachments during 1915 and 1916.

By 1917 the primary weapon of the King's African Rifles was the .303in Short Magazine Lee Enfield (SMLE) Mk III rifle. The SMLE Mk III had been introduced to service in 1907 along with the Pattern 1907 sword bayonet. It had a muzzle velocity of 2,441ft/sec, an effective firing range of 550yd and a maximum range of 3,000yd, and used a ten-round magazine loaded with five-round charger clips. The SMLE Mk III weighed 8.8lb and was 44in long. Its shorter length made it far handier in the bush than the longer Lee-Enfields and Lee-Metfords with which the King's African Rifles had been armed at the start of the war.

Beginning in 1916, King's African Rifles battalions were reorganized to parallel standard British infantry structure. These battalions each had four rifle companies and one machine-gun section with four Vickers machine guns. On paper, a King's African Rifles battalion counted over 1,000 men. Once in the field, however, the actual numbers were fewer as sickness, battle casualties, injuries and detachment for other duties eroded the battalion strength. For example, in August 1917 1/2nd KAR counted 68 Europeans and 690 Africans. In contrast to other theatres, where machine guns were removed and grouped into machine-gun companies, King's African Rifles battalions retained organic Vickers machine guns. The importance of tripod-mounted heavy machine guns in the East African bush resulted in the King's African Rifles battalion's machine-gun section being expanded into a machine-gun half-company with eight Vickers guns in June 1917. In theory, a European NCO was to be in charge of each Vickers gun, this being based on the belief that Europeans were more capable of directing the guns in action. In 1917 each rifle company

Britain's heavy machine gun in the war was the tripod-mounted Vickers Mk I that fired a 0.303in bullet. The basic machine-gun design was used by both the British and the Germans, having been invented by Hiram Maxim, an American. The British gun was officially the 'Gun, Machine, Mark I, Vickers 0.303 inch' as adopted on 26 November 1912. The Vickers was mounted on a heavy tripod and required a six-man crew. When set up for battle, it weighed 99lb, including the gun, cooling water and tripod. The ammunition was fed by a belt-feed system with each belt having 250 rounds. The gun's rate of fire was 450–600rds/min and an ammunition box of full belts weighed 22lb. In 1914, two Vickers guns were part of a first-line British infantry battalion, or roughly one Vickers per 400 rifles. The King's African Rifles allocated one Vickers gun per rifle company, a ratio of one gun per 100 rifles. This liberal allotment was based on past experience of East African bush fighting and the deployment of individual companies in isolated garrisons across British territories. The Vickers served to offset the numerical weakness of the King's African Rifles compared to larger indigenous tribal forces. (© IWM Q 71253)

received two light machine guns, the famed Lewis gun. In 1918, the number of Lewis guns within a company was increased to four, providing one to each platoon. The Lewis gun revolutionized infantry tactics by providing mobile automatic firepower that could accompany attacking infantry, and it became an integral component of the King's African Rifles' organization and tactics.

The King's African Rifles was on the offensive in 1917 and 1918, the result being that many of the fights in which they participated were encounter battles when the British came upon a German force which frequently was in an entrenched position on ground of the Germans' choice. Rapid deployment of a firing line was important. Single file, and sometimes four abreast, was the easiest way to move along trails in the bush, but unfortunately was not suited to rapid deployment. Formations were adapted to the terrain and a special 'bush formation' came into use. A typical bush formation had a battalion marching in a line of companies. The companies would deploy platoons in parallel with troops deployed as flankers on each side of the company. The leading company deployed a line of soldiers across its front with 6–8yd between individuals. Each soldier would have to cut his way through the bush – and the going could be slow through heavy bush. Slow progress of a force on an extended front in the bush would frequently cause commanders to chance moving in single column to gain speed.

Once the enemy was encountered, an attacking commander needed to determine if he was facing a delaying detail or had run into a German defensive position. The usual response was to deploy only a firing line sufficiently strong to force the enemy to reveal his position while sending patrols out to find his flanks. While this was happening, the column would

The Stokes Gun, better known as the 3in Stokes mortar, was basically a smoothbore metal tube attached to a plate on the bottom and elevated by means of a bipod mount fixed to its front. A shell was dropped down the tube (muzzle loaded) and the shell's base would impact a fixed firing pin at the base that would detonate the propellant charge. Although designated as being a '3in mortar', the Stokes actually had a 3.2in bore. The mortar weighed 104lb, required a crew of two, and fired a high-explosive shell that weighed 10lb 11oz with a sustained rate of fire of 8rds/min at an effective range of about 750yd. The ability to get a Stokes mortar into action quickly and its light weight made it a valuable addition to the British arsenal; and its short range and high angle of fire made it an excellent weapon for bush fighting. Initially used by European troops or detachments from the West Indies Regiment, it became available to support the King's African Rifles in 1917. During the last months of 1917 the King's African Rifles acquired Stokes mortars and integrated these into its organization at the brigade/column level. Batteries of six mortars were usually assigned to each of the principal columns, while smaller columns would each have a section of two mortars. If available, a Stokes mortar would be placed with the advance troops. In 1918, Stokes mortars were frequently attached to individual King's African Rifles battalions, and by the end of the war had replaced the mountain gun as the primary indirect-fire weapon in East Africa's bush. (© IWM ORD 27)

keep most of the force out of the fight and prepare for a possible enemy counter-attack. Generally, the heavy machine guns were placed in the centre of a company's deployment with the lighter Lewis guns sent to the flank. Firefights in the bush could last for hours but with relatively few casualties being suffered, especially by a defender fighting from prepared positions.

Once the enemy's position was known, an attack would be conducted as fast as possible to avoid letting the troops stop to establish another firing line, which would result in the attack stalling as they would frequently be lying down and firing from a prone position with enemy fire passing overhead. Whenever possible, an attack would target the enemy's flank. Since the Germans would usually counter-attack, a commander would seek to maintain a strong reserve in hand. With limited visibility in the bush, an enemy counter-attack could come from almost any direction, so maintaining this reserve was critical.

When present, artillery would be deployed to shell the enemy's position. The most effective artillery units were Indian mountain batteries. These guns would sometimes be manhandled to the front and used for direct fire, with German machine-gun positions being a favourite target. The limited amount

of artillery available to both sides, and the problems of transporting guns in a climate that killed draught animals, resulted in machine guns being far more dominant on the battlefields of East Africa than artillery pieces. In 1917 and 1918 British artillery, when present, was on the scale of one or two batteries per brigade-sized column.

Schutztruppe

The Schutztruppe started and ended the war with one official organization for combat units. Throughout the war, the Germans continued to adapt and adjust organizations to the local military needs and the environment. The *Feldkompagnie* was the largest formal unit in the Schutztruppe and was designed as an independent, self-contained, mobile combat unit. The pre-war strength of the *Feldkompagnie* was 16 to 20 European officers and senior NCOs (including medical and non-combatant personnel), two African officers called *effendis* (a holdover from the 1880s and 1890s when Sudanese made up the majority of the force) and up to 200 askaris. As the war progressed, *Feldkompagnien* decreased in size. In 1917 many companies were averaging ten Europeans and 100 to 120 askaris, but the basic organization remained the same. A dedicated carrier unit of up to 250 carriers was associated with each *Feldkompagnie* and during the war these carriers would sometimes provide new recruits to replace losses within a company. When multiple companies were required to operate together, they were grouped into an *Abteilung* that was usually known by the commander's name. (When translated into English, *Abteilung* is frequently rendered as 'detachment'.)

Some Schutztruppe units were equipped with the rifle (Gewehr 98) or carbine (Karabiner 98) versions of the Mauser 98. There were 579 of the rifles and 1,676 of the carbines in German East Africa in August 1914; these equipped European personnel (including settler volunteers) and six of the *Feldkompagnien*. The Mauser 98 fired a 7.92mm round and was a bolt-action weapon with a five-round magazine. In 1915, 1,800 Mauser Gewehr 98s were brought in by the blockade-runner *Rubens*.

A European infantry unit hastily deploys in the East African bush. Regardless of the origins of the infantryman, he had to deal with the same environmental conditions and terrain in East Africa. The bush made movement difficult and frequently hid an enemy lying in ambush or moving around one's flanks. Small-unit leadership was the critical level of command in combat because restricted lines of sight and primitive communications resulted in dispersed units that could not be controlled centrally. Many times the decisions and actions of a platoon NCO or section leader would determine the outcome of a firefight. (Photo by The Print Collector/Print Collector/Getty Images)

19

The predominant German machine gun by 1914 was the water-cooled Maschinengewehr 08 (MG 08), firing a 7.92mm round with a rate of fire of 500–600rds/min, though the need to change the 250-round fabric belts would reduce this rate in the field. Its effective firing range was 2,000m (2,185ft) and its maximum range was 3,500m (3,825yd). Total weight of an MG 08 with cooling water was approximately 69kg (152lb), with the gun itself weighing 26kg (58lb) and the tripod mount 39kg (85lb). Each Schutztruppe *Feldkompagnie* had two or three MG 08s, each requiring a four-man crew to operate it. (© BArch, Bild 105-DOA6744 / Dobbertin, Walther I 1914/1918 ca.)

The remaining eight pre-war *Feldkompagnien* were armed with the Mauser M1871/84 (M71) Jägerbüsche which fired an 11mm bullet using black powder for its propellant, with the result that the M71 left a conspicuous cloud of smoke when fired. Against pre-war African opponents this had not been a problem. When fighting an opponent deploying modern weapons and tactics, however, the black-powder smoke clouds gave away the firers' positions. There were 10,507 M71 rifles in German East Africa in August 1914, making it the most common German rifle at the start of the war.

Throughout the campaign the Schutztruppe replaced its M71s with captured Allied rifles whenever possible. During operations in Portuguese East Africa, large numbers of modern rifles, usually called the Portuguese Mauser, were captured. This was officially the Mauser-Vergueiro: a bolt-action rifle designed and developed from the Mauser 98 rifle in 1904 by José Alberto Vergueiro, an infantry officer of the Portuguese Army. The Portuguese Mauser fired a 6.5mm bullet that had been specially designed for it, weighed 8.4lb, was

The double-rank firing line was a pre-war tactical staple of both the Schutztruppe (shown here) and the King's African Rifles. Against local opposition frequently armed with spears and muzzle-loading muskets, the classic infantry line and the infantry square were effective tactics in the bush; but officers in both colonies were well aware that they could not fight a modern foe using these archaic formations. Before 1914, both the King's African Rifles and the Schutztruppe had developed plans for defending their colonies and bush tactics to use if a European war came to East Africa. (© BArch, Bild 105-DOA6749 / Walther Dobbertin)

The Germans formed artillery batteries and half-batteries during the war. These were ad hoc units armed with a variety of guns. The majority of artillery pieces in the colony were obsolescent or else light guns intended for colonial operations. In 1914 the Schutztruppe's artillery consisted of 11 9cm Krupp C73 field guns such as this one, plus two 6cm, three 4.7cm, 11 3.7cm and eight 3.7cm revolving cannon. During the war two 6cm and two 7.5cm cannon and four 10.5cm light howitzers reached German East Africa aboard supply ships that ran the British blockade. By summer 1917, the Schutztruppe was reduced to two converted 10.5cm *Königsberg* guns, two 10.5cm howitzers, two 7.5cm cannon and one each of the following: C73, 6cm, 4.7cm and 3.7cm cannon. There was also one captured Portuguese mountain gun. (Captured artillery pieces were used when ammunition for them was available.) In most cases artillery pieces were employed singularly, with the lighter pieces used for direct fire. German artillerymen in East Africa did not have the capabilities or the opportunities to become the battle-dominating force that their cousins in Europe were afforded during the war. (Photo by Henry Guttmann/ Getty Images)

43.3in long, was sighted for ranges from 200yd to 2,000yd (effective range was 500–600yd) and had a muzzle velocity of 2,346ft/sec. Its feed system used a five-round clip that fed an internal box magazine. By November 1918 about two-thirds of Schutztruppe rifles were captured Portuguese Mausers.

The Schutztruppe's firepower was based on the machine gun, of which the Germans had 67 in East Africa in August 1914. Since the early days of German East Africa the tripod-mounted heavy machine gun had been a critical component of the Schutztruppe, compensating for their numerical weakness compared to potential rebellious indigenous forces. These guns were the foundation of their tactics because experience had shown that rifle fire was usually too high in the bush. The heavy machine gun mounted on its tripod provided a stable weapon that could be used literally to sweep the ground in front of it with a hail of bullets. Because of the weapon's stability, the gunner could reliably aim his fire secure in the knowledge that he would cover the desired fire zone; and by using the gun's calibrated sights he could decrease or increase the range at which the bullets would be effective. Despite personnel losses, machine-gun teams were kept up to strength. By the end of the war, companies counted fewer than 100 askaris but still manned two or three machine guns each.

Given the strategic situation, German forces were generally on the defensive. Schutztruppe defensive tactics were not static, however, but were based on the concept of an active defence. Lettow-Vorbeck was always seeking a battle to inflict maximum damage upon British forces, especially any isolated units he could trap. Using prepared defensive positions that relied on machines guns to achieve economy of force, the Schutztruppe tried to keep the maximum number of troops available for counter-attacks. Rapid and hard-hitting counter-attacks were the staple of the German defence. Counter-attacks were usually directed at the flanks of the attackers, although sometimes the counter-attackers would attempt to go around the British front and attack forces behind the front such as supporting artillery, reserves and supply trains. The longer-range flanking attacks often included machine guns that would add to the chaos and confusion

This plate shows an askari private in action during a firefight against the King's African Rifles near Lioma, Portuguese East Africa, in late August 1918. He and his comrades have been in the field, marching almost daily during Lettow-Vorbeck's raid-like invasion of Portuguese territory. The British sea blockade of German East Africa has forced the Schutztruppe to improvise much of their equipment. Repairing worn garments, and using captured Allied clothing, weapons, ammunitions and other supplies became a way of life for the roving brigade that represented Germany's last military force in Africa.

Weapons, dress and equipment

Stocks of the Portuguese Mauser rifle (**1**) were captured from the Portuguese, who by default had become the unwilling suppliers of Lettow-Vorbeck's force. By the late summer of 1918 over 1,000 Schutztruppe askaris were armed with these rifles.

This askari is wearing a civilian-style bush or safari hat (**2**); the shortage of regulation-issue equipment resulted in adaptations of and deviations in uniform that German commanders accepted as a necessity of war. His pre-war uniform tunic (**3**) has been patched and shows evidence of the wear and tear of years of use, as do his trousers (**4**). His pre-war-issue blue-coloured puttees (**5**) remain, but he now wears captured British brown leather ammunition boots (**6**) in place of worn-out pre-war-issued German regulation footwear.

A pair of pre-war leather straps and a belt allows him to carry six cartridge pouches (**7**) around his waist, while a separate strap carries his bread bag (**8**) that also serves as a haversack. A pre-war-issued water bottle (**9**) is attached to his belt. A bayonet for his Mauser-Vergueiro rifle remains in its bayonet holder (**10**) because, as with the King's African Rifles, the confining space in bush fighting for manoeuvring one's rifle resulted in the bayonet only being fitted just before a bayonet charge. The askari is not carrying a pack or a bed roll: in the Schutztruppe these items, weighing up to 25lb, were carried by indigenous porters of the *Feldkompagnie's* first-line supply trains when it was in the field.

After the cruiser *Königsberg* was sunk in the shallow waters of the Rufigi River, its 8.8cm and 10.5cm guns were salvaged by the Schutztruppe, converted to land use and manned by naval crews. Several guns were emplaced in fixed defences; the others were mounted on improvised gun carriages and converted into improvised heavy field artillery. The gun crews came from the marooned gunners of the *Königsberg*. The British initially did not have any artillery to match these guns until they too improvised long-range artillery from naval guns and in 1916 brought in a battery of 5.5in howitzers. (© BArch, Bild 134-C0318 / Dobbertin, Walther I 1915)

in a British force suddenly set upon by a violent attack in an area that had been thought of as being behind the line. Frequently, a British flank attack would run head-on into a German counter-attack, with both forces coming to a halt and the action dissolving into a chaotic short-range firefight.

LOGISTICS

Supply and transport determined the course of the campaign in East Africa for both sides. The local environment did not readily support living off the land, and the primitive transportation system exacerbated the difficulties involved in moving supplies up to the combat forces. These difficulties were compounded by problems associated with water: too much in the rainy season led to widespread flooding; too little in the dry season resulted in water holes being unable to meet the needs of front-line troops.

Agriculture, which was nearly at subsistence level in many areas, was barely able to feed the local population. As a result, there were few locations where a force could live off the land for any length of time. The Germans organized food-supply depots within their colony from the start of the war and secured those areas where crops were plentiful. Schutztruppe units would operate in these regions to guard the harvest and ensure that it went to replenish their stores. In 1917 the British recognized the importance of these depots and food-producing regions and included their capture or destruction among their objectives. As German forces withdrew from areas they systematically stripped food supplies to feed their forces and deny foraging to the advancing enemy, thus complicating the British supply problems. Hunting quickly became a necessity to supply protein instead of being a sport, and good hunters were valuable assets to both the Schutztruppe and the King's African Rifles in the field. Memoirs of participants frequently describe meals where fresh game was a welcome treat for hungry men.

East Africa was an undeveloped region with no munitions industry, so the tools of modern warfare had to be shipped in from overseas. Cut off from Europe by the Royal Navy's blockade, the Germans in East Africa had to make best use of what stockpiles they had at the start of the war and whatever they could improvise. Britain's control of the oceans allowed munitions and matériel from around the world to be brought into any suitable port, thus allowing British forces close to ports to be relatively well supplied.

Once forces moved inland from the coast of German East Africa, there was no extensive rail network like that in Western Europe. The roads that existed were not much more than tracks; and even where roads did exist, draught animals died off rapidly due to animal diseases carried by the tsetse fly. The British offensive of 1916 came to a halt when the animal-dependent transport system collapsed. Mechanical transport, light trucks in particular, offered an alternative that was exploited by the British in 1917 and 1918 – but trucks required roads, and combat units soon found road construction in the bush to be a standard procedure and part of operations on the march.

Even with light trucks in use, the final stages of supply movement relied on African human carriers for transport. This limited the distance that forces

A mechanical transport convoy of the Royal Flying Corps near the Ruwu River in April 1917. The British attempt to use traditional draught-animal transport to supply their forces during the 1916 offensive had failed miserably due to fly-borne animal diseases. Light trucks were the solution for getting supplies from ports and railheads forward to field depots, where indigenous human carriers took over the task of serving as first-line transport. The large ration strength of white personnel in East Africa in 1917 and 1918 was primarily from motor-transport and other technical-service units, and not combat troops. (© IWM Q 15589)

Both sides were forced to use large numbers of indigenous human carriers to move supplies to forward units. The Germans established depots behind their lines and used local carrier relays to move supplies. Each Schutztruppe unit included a dedicated organic carrier group which received some training and served as a limited source of replacement askaris. The King's African Rifles created a special corps of machine-gun carriers; frequently these men stood by their machine guns in combat and fought and died beside the gun crews. (© BArch, Bild 105-DOA6448 / Dobbertin, Walther I1906/14 ca.)

could operate from a supply base or road head since the carrier had to be fed, which meant he had to carry his own food in addition to the supplies he carried for the troops. The number of carriers needed was significant: one British estimate gave a number of 13,700 carriers to supply a force of three battalions located inland. Availability of carriers was a continual problem. The British prohibited the wives of their carriers from accompanying the supply columns, resulting in greater difficulty recruiting and keeping carriers who, once in the field, would leave and try to return home to their families. The Germans, despite efforts to stop the practice in the final phase of the campaign, permitted the wives of askaris and carriers to accompany their columns.

LEADERSHIP, RECRUITMENT AND LOYALTY

When the war started, the King's African Rifles' leadership model was based on European officers and African NCOs plus a limited number of African officers (mostly Sudanese). This model had been true since the beginning of the King's African Rifles; in 1902 3rd Battalion, KAR, comprising eight companies, was authorized to have 25 European officers. Pre-war King's African Rifles officers were volunteers on detached duty from their parent regiments for a two- to three-year tour in East Africa. A company in the field could be led by a single junior British officer. Command depended on British company-grade officers issuing verbal orders to African NCOs, either in English or an indigenous language; the NCO then directed the askaris to carry out their tasks. During the years preceding the war, units of the King's African Rifles and its predecessors had served on internal-security duties in East Africa, including Somaliland, and had been sent to West Africa to serve in the Ashanti Campaign and Gambia Expeditions in 1900–01. None of these operations gave the British any reason to add European NCOs to the force.

In contrast, the German Schutztruppe had from its inception included a significant contingent of European NCOs within its ranks. German officers and NCOs were volunteers from the Imperial Army. Officers were required to have at least three years' experience while NCOs required a total of three years' service with one year as an NCO. Both had to pass a detailed medical examination. Initial service tours in German East Africa were 2½ years with an option for extending. Learning their askaris' languages was required. The Germans quickly utilized their local European personnel, many of whom were veterans who had settled in German East Africa at the end of their service, as officers and NCOs for the Schutztruppe. Unlike the British, who allowed East African European volunteer units to remain intact and wither away, the Germans amalgamated European volunteer settler units into the Schutztruppe organization. This move permitted the Germans to maintain a high percentage of Europeans within all the companies, generally a ratio of one European to ten Africans. Throughout the war, the Germans tried to maintain this ratio in their units and keep the

Askaris of 1st Battalion, KAR in January 1916. This battalion was recruited in the Nyasaland Protectorate, a region that provided an excellent recruiting ground for the King's African Rifles. The soldiers shown here may be some of the new recruits raised in late 1915. One call for 500 recruits to serve in British East Africa resulted in 984 new soldiers and 180 veterans being sent to Kenya, a result that surprised Colonial officials. By early 1916, companies of 1st Battalion, KAR were scattered from Northern Rhodesia to Kenya. The companies in British East Africa became the cadres upon which 2nd Battalion, KAR was re-established in early 1916 with the above 1,164 men from Nyasaland. These two battalions, recruited in Nyasaland, were each subsequently expanded into a four-battalion regiment during the war. (Photo by Culture Club/Getty Images)

OPPOSITE A German colonist departing for war. Probably posed for propaganda value, this image illustrates the German mobilization of colonial settlers. The white-manned *Schützenkompagnien* formed in 1914 were soon reorganized, and by 1917 had only minor differences in manpower and organization from Schutztruppe *Feldkompagnien*. The reservists and members of volunteer rifle clubs were the sources for European officers, NCOs and specialists that the rapid expansion of the Schutztruppe required. (© BArch, Bild 105-DOA7346 / Walther Dobbertin)

Europeans within the same *Feldkompagnie* as a means to increase unit cohesion. Transfers were limited to replacing lost leaders or when units were combined because of losses. Front-line leadership by example was a Schutztruppe standard, but it led to heavy losses of European officers and NCOs.

British leaders attributed the battlefield performance of the Schutztruppe to its higher proportion of Europeans compared to the proportion of such men in the King's African Rifles. As a result the British strove to increase the proportion of European officers and NCOs on the regiment's rolls. Initially, new officers and NCOs were recruited from Europeans in Africa, i.e. surviving members of the East African Mounted Rifles, the Rhodesian Regiment and a few from South African units. Later, officers and NCOs were brought in from other fronts, resulting in a mixture of adventurous volunteers and cast-offs from other units. Many received little training before being posted to King's African Rifles units in the field; in some instances British officers and NCOs were thrown into combat with no knowledge of their askaris' indigenous language, thus placing a greater burden upon the indigenous NCOs. On both sides European officers and NCOs led by example, resulting in heavy casualties. Accounts of actions between the King's African Rifles and its Schutztruppe opponents frequently cite a shortage of European personnel, resulting in African NCOs and ordinary askaris using their initiative and leading their fellow Africans in battle.

Service in either the King's African Rifles or the Schutztruppe represented a chance for an African to be employed in a relatively high-paying job with a degree of job security and privileges. The attraction of pre-war service as a soldier was demonstrated when 2nd Battalion, KAR was disbanded in 1911. Many askaris deemed redundant and discharged by the British as a result of the battalion's disbandment simply went across the colonial border and enlisted in the Schutztruppe.

During the war the two sides ended up following different paths when it came to recruiting Africans to serve as soldiers. The Schutztruppe expanded during 1914 and 1915, but thereafter undertook little recruitment to replace losses. Some captured Allied askaris chose to change sides and enlist in the Schutztruppe, and occasionally African carriers of long service were permitted to enlist in the *Feldkompagnie* to which they were attached. The British undertook extensive recruitment of new askaris throughout the war, especially after the sudden expansion of the King's African Rifles in 1916. As the war in East Africa progressed, British recruitment of African soldiers was aided by the Allies' policy of extensive conscription of carriers for their supply service. For a healthy African, service in the King's African Rifles (or other African units) offered better pay, privileges and conditions than service in the carrier corps. The British also utilized captured askaris, to the degree that the rank and file of 6th KAR was predominantly made up of former Schutztruppe askari veterans.

On both sides the high pay offered to askaris when compared to that of civilian jobs, their unique privileges and the conscious efforts made by officials to cultivate a feeling of higher social status than that of the surrounding civilian population resulted in the askaris showing a high degree of loyalty to their unit and their officers. This loyalty was based on traditional African concepts and not a love of the colonial power. In the final analysis, African loyalty was based on self-interest and could frequently depend on which side was perceived by the African to be winning at the time.

Narunyu

18 August 1917

BACKGROUND TO BATTLE

The 1917 British dry-season offensive in south-eastern German East Africa started with attacks conducted by forces operating from the Indian Ocean port of Kilwa in July. By the end of the month the Kilwa force was facing stiffer resistance and making little progress. South of Kilwa was a British force at the Indian Ocean port of Lindi. Designated Linforce, it had been ordered only to patrol and defend Lindi during July; but in late July its commander,

Linforce's reason for being: the port at Lindi. Here replacements for the Nigerian Brigade can be seen coming ashore. Lindi, along with other ports on the southern coast of German East Africa, was occupied by British forces in late 1916 in order to deny them to German blockade-runners and provide locations for the Royal Navy and Merchant Marine to land supplies for advancing British troops. Despite the primitive port facilities at Lindi and Kilwa, both became major bases for van Deventer's forces in 1917. (© IWM Q 15370)

George Giffard

George Giffard (27 September 1886–17 November 1964) was commissioned in 1906 in The Queen's (Royal West Surrey Regiment). In 1913 he was seconded to the King's African Rifles and by the start of the war was OC B Company, 1st Battalion, KAR, deployed in Kenya. In January 1915 he led his company, plus three companies of 3rd Battalion, KAR, in action against the Schutztruppe at Jassin on the coast of German East Africa. By March 1916 Giffard was commanding a four-company detachment of the King's African Rifles stationed in Kenya during the main British attack under Lt-Gen Jan Christiaan Smuts. After a month these four companies were withdrawn and used as the nucleus of the re-formed 2nd Battalion, KAR in Nairobi.

Giffard was appointed as 2IC 2nd Battalion, KAR in April 1916. When the battalion was split into 1/2nd and 2/2nd KAR, Giffard, now a major, was 2IC 1/2nd KAR. On 24 October 1916 he became CO 1/2nd KAR. He led the battalion through the 1917 campaign having been promoted to lieutenant-colonel. After the bloody fighting at Nyangao/Mahiwa, 1/2nd KAR and 3/2nd KAR were temporarily consolidated into one battalion which Giffard commanded. At the end of November 1917 he was transferred to the

King's African Rifles headquarters in Nairobi. In February 1918, now 31 years old and a colonel, Giffard returned to the field to take command of 1st Brigade KAR, made up of battalions of 2nd KAR. The name of Giffard's brigade soon became KARTUCOL, for KAR 2nd (Regiment) Column. Under Giffard's command, KARTUCOL became a crack force respected by Lettow-Vorbeck. An Australian big-game hunter turned intelligence scout in East Africa described George Giffard (although misspelling his name) and KARTUCOL in 1918: 'Colonel Gifford himself, an efficient and tireless soldier, expected his officers and men to be the same. Cool and collected in any engagement, he was, as I have said, with his column, our one redeeming feature in this 1918 campaign in P.E.A. ... without Colonel Gifford and the K.A.R. 2nd Col. it might easily have been almost disastrous' (Wienholt 1922: 237).

During World War II, Giffard – now a full general – was GOC 11th Army Group in South East Asia during 1943–44. General (later Field Marshal) Sir William Slim, GOC Fourteenth Army, served under Giffard and recorded in his memoirs that Giffard had been an excellent superior and that his departure was viewed with regret by the army.

Brig-Gen Henry de Courcy O'Grady, sent a memorandum to van Deventer listing four reasons for changing the main axis of advance from Kilwa to Lindi. First, all available information indicated that Lettow-Vorbeck was planning to retire to the border with Portuguese East Africa. Second,

Kurt Wahle

On 2 August 1914 retired Saxon Generalmajor Kurt Wahle stepped ashore at Dar es Salaam on a visit to his son who had settled in German East Africa; but what was to have been a holiday turned into four years of active service as Wahle became one of the senior officers of the Schutztruppe during World War I. Once war was declared, Wahle promptly volunteered his services to Lettow-Vorbeck and was placed in charge of organizing the lines of communications for defending the colony. In May 1915, Wahle was sent to the south-western portion of the colony bordering Northern Rhodesia and Nyasaland to command a force of four *Feldkompagnien* (18., 23., 24. and 29. FK) plus half of 10. SchK and two Krupp C73 cannon against local British forces.

In preparing to resist the British and Belgian offensive in 1916 in the north-western and western parts of German East Africa, a single German field command was created. Wahle was appointed to the post of Westbefehlshaber with headquarters at Tabora, German East Africa. Although

forced to retire by virtue of the weight of Belgian and British numbers, he was able to maintain the core of an effective field force. He continued in this position until recalled in May 1917 and posted to command the forces against Linforce. Following the hard fighting of the dry season of 1917 and Lettow-Vorbeck's pruning of the Schutztruppe in November of that year, Wahle remained in the field. He commanded a battalion-sized *Abteilung* during the first nine months of 1918. Finally, in September 1918, suffering from a double hernia, he stayed behind as the Schutztruppe moved on and was captured by the British, who treated him with great respect.

Generalmajor Kurt Wahle was awarded the Iron Cross 1st Class and the Pour le Mérite during the war. He had the distinction of being the oldest active combatant in the war. Additionally, he probably commanded the most unusual force led by a German general in the field – a single Schutztruppe company and approximately 200 indigenous irregulars – during one action in 1915.

A King's African Rifles column crossing a river. The lack of roads resulted in riverbanks becoming trails by virtue of necessity. Using a river as a march route could result in frequent crossing of the waters as the banks changed from firm ground to swamps. This image illustrates what it would have been like for soldiers of Linforce moving along the Lukuledi River. (Photo by: Universal History Archive/UIG via Getty Images)

advancing from Kilwa would merely press Lettow-Vorbeck back in the direction he wished to proceed. Third, a British advance from Lindi would be along a shorter road and might cut off Lettow-Vorbeck from his accumulated supplies in the south of the colony. Finally, O'Grady believed that threatening the Germans' southern route might bring on a decisive battle. Van Deventer agreed with O'Grady's concept and decided to reinforce Linforce, directing it to plan an attack for early August.

Linforce had six infantry battalions available for mobile operations with a fighting strength of 236 officers and NCOs and 3,226 enlisted men armed with 34 machine guns and 48 Lewis guns; 1,980 of the men were askaris of 1/2nd, 3/2nd and 3/4th KAR. Opposing these battalions was Abt Wahle, consisting of eight companies – 4. SchK, 9. FK, 16. FK, 19. FK, 20. FK, 'Tanga' Kompagnie, 'O' Kompagnie and 'S' Kompagnie – with a fighting strength of 120 Europeans and 1,200 Africans armed with 20 machine guns. This force was commanded by one of Lettow-Vorbeck's more unusual subordinates, Generalmajor Kurt Wahle.

Linforce attacked on 3 August and was repulsed with roughly 500 casualties. After receiving a report about this action, van Deventer ordered Linforce to outflank the enemy's position by means of a turning movement. This manoeuvre was to use the Lukuledi River valley to seize a position astride the Germans' line of communications while a second British force demonstrated against the German positions. O'Grady organized two columns: the flanking column (1/2nd KAR, 8th South African Infantry and two companies of 3/4th KAR), commanded by Lt-Col A.J. Taylor, CO 8th South African Infantry; and the main column (25th Royal Fusiliers, 3/2nd KAR, Kashmir Mountain Battery and a Stokes mortar battery) under O'Grady's personal command. These columns totalled 2,010 rifles, 1,650 of whom were King's African Rifles askaris. With sickness rapidly eroding the European and Indian battalions, the King's African Rifles was providing the majority of the British infantry.

During the afternoon of 9 August, Taylor's column started its march, crossing the Lukuledi River to move along its right (south-eastern) bank and camping east of the German defence line. Taylor's column continued its march on 10 August; meeting no opposition, it reached a position about 1 mile east of Narunyu and entrenched for the night. During the night of 10/11 August, Abt Wahle withdrew to Narunyu on the Lukuledi. After receiving reports of the 3 August fighting and British losses, Lettow-Vorbeck decided to march to the Lindi area with five companies and two half-batteries of artillery. In his typical fashion, Lettow-Vorbeck was seeking a surprise concentration of troops in order to inflict a major tactical defeat upon a detached British force.

O'Grady's column joined Taylor's camped east of Narunyu, but heavy rains for the next five days forced a halt to major operations until the area dried out. During this halt, British reconnaissance patrols scouted the Narunyu position. Their reports showed the position would be difficult to attack. Narunyu was located in river-bottom lands on the north bank of the Lukuledi. Immediately north-west an escarpment rose 150ft, south were swamps of the Lukuledi, while to the east was a dense sisal plantation. Trenches ran up against the escarpment and there were trenches in the dense bush on its top.

Wahle deployed his force as follows: on the right flank Abt Kraut held the line from the Lukuledi River to the escarpment with 20. FK, 'O' Kompagnie and 'S' Kompagnie; the left flank (atop the escarpment) was Abt Rothe with 19. FK and 'Tanga' Kompagnie; in reserve were 9. FK and 4. SchK. Meanwhile 16. FK, which had been part of Wahle's command a few days previously, appears to have been posted on Ruho Ridge south of the Lukuledi. Lettow-Vorbeck with 3. FK and 11. FK was within 8 miles of Narunyu.

O'Grady decided to flank the Germans from the north on the high ground above the Lukuledi River bottom. A flanking force would cut its way through the bush using compass bearings to reach a position that overlooked the enemy's defences. Taylor would command the turning movement with 1/2nd KAR, the company-strength 25th Royal Fusiliers, and a two-gun section of Stokes mortars; 3/4th KAR would demonstrate against the eastern face of the Narunyu defences with two companies and Ruho Ridge with its other two companies. O'Grady's artillery (the Kashmir Mountain Battery and one section of 27th Mountain Battery) would bombard the front of the position. In reserve, 3/2nd KAR, 8th South African Infantry and the remaining two sections (four guns) of Stokes mortars were to follow up the success of Taylor's column. The rains having ceased, Taylor's troops moved out late on 17 August. Led by 1/2nd KAR, the flanking column headed north and then north-west until it reached a light-railway line (used by planters to move their harvests to Lindi) on the flat ground, where the troops stopped for a few hours' rest before proceeding.

This photograph shows part of the Nigerian Brigade marching cross-country in scrub-covered terrain. This is similar to the scrub through which Lt-Col A.J. Taylor's column, led by 1/2nd KAR, marched during 18 August to approach Narunyu. Although the column's advance appears to have been slow to anyone who has not seen or experienced trying to move through this terrain on foot, it must be remembered that it was necessary to cut a path through such dense scrub. (© IWM Q 15397)

MAP KEY

1 **Before dawn:** Lt-Col A.J. Taylor's column starts its flank march.

2 *c.***0830hrs:** After marching 6,250yd through the dense bush, Taylor's column stops for a short rest.

3 **0930hrs:** Moving south, and once again experiencing slow going, Taylor's column discovers a newly cut road through the bush.

4 *c.***1000hrs:** 3/4th KAR demonstrates against the German positions.

5 *c.***1030hrs:** 1/2nd KAR deploys astride a road in bush formation; dense bush forces it back into march order at 1230hrs.

6 **1300hrs:** 1/2nd KAR encounters Abt Rothe and deploys a firing line.

7 **1330–1400hrs:** 4. SchK attempts a flank attack; A Company, 1/2nd KAR stops it.

8 **After 1400hrs:** German forces attacking from the west are stopped by D Company, 1/2nd KAR.

9 *c.***1500hrs:** 9. FK is committed.

10 *c.***1500hrs:** 25th Royal Fusiliers establishes a position 600yd behind 1/2nd KAR.

11 *c.***1700hrs:** A company of 3/2nd KAR reinforces 1/2nd KAR.

12 **1800hrs:** 1/2nd KAR withdraws, joining 25th Royal Fusiliers.

13 *c.***1900hrs:** 3. FK and 11. FK commence multiple attacks lasting until about 2000hrs.

14 **2100–2200hrs:** Covered by heavy fire the Schutztruppe retire.

Battlefield environment

In 1917, Narunyu sat in the river-bottom lands on the north side of the Lukuledi River. The river-bottom lands were covered with marshes and swamps except for the ground that had been cleared, drained and used to plant sisal. To the north-west, a steep slope rose 150ft to drier land where the fighting occurred. Here was black cotton soil which, with a clay content of roughly one-third, becomes very hard when dry and very sticky when wet. This soil is unstable and inhospitable to many species of trees, but good for scrub bush.

In the area of Narunyu the foliage was closed-scrub 7–26ft high, with dense foliage covering 70–100 per cent of an area. This resulted in short ranges for vision, compelling a force to move cautiously into essentially unknown territory. Defenders had a natural advantage in a firefight owing to their ability to ambush an attacker. The Germans had prepared their position with trenches and constructed a cleared trail through the bush, referred to by the British as the 'new-cut road', on the high ground west and north of Narunyu. Led by 1/2nd KAR, Taylor's column experienced slow going, having to hack a path through the dense bush until intersecting this road. Even then, the dense bush prevented the force from moving in bush formation and retarded the advance until it struck the German defences.

Based on the dark colour of their shirts, this picture shows a South African infantry unit moving through rugged, scrub-covered land. This type of terrain provided a defender with innumerable opportunities to surprise an advancing enemy. At the same time, however, the bush could hide an advancing enemy unless the approaches to a defensive position were cleared – but cleared fields of fire would in turn alert the enemy to the possibility that an opponent was in position on the other side of the clearing. This led to many close-range firefights. (Photo by The Print Collector/Print Collector/Getty Images)

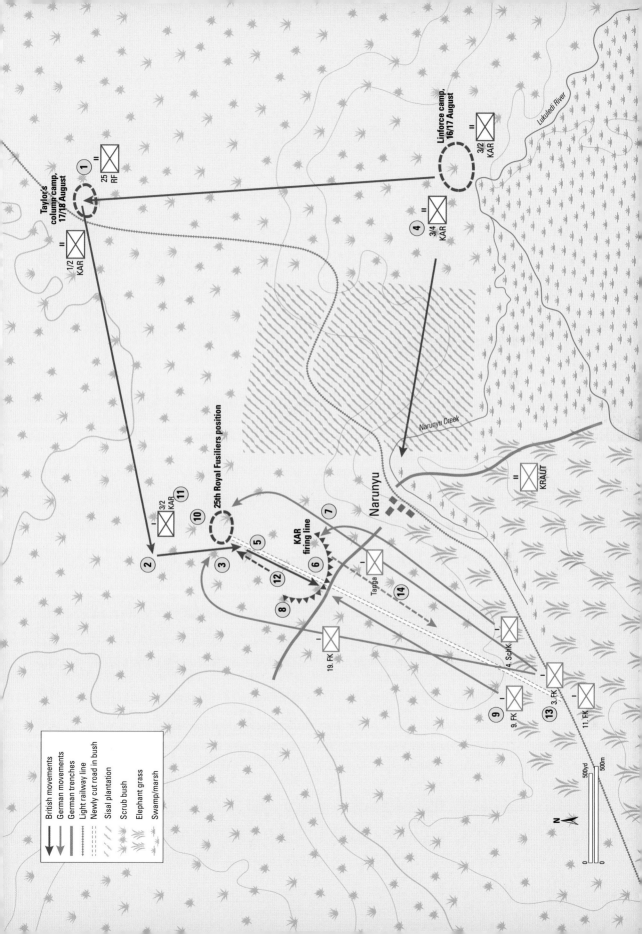

Taylor's
column camp,
17/18 August

Linforce camp,
16/17 August

① 25
RF

= 3/2
KAR

= 3/4
KAR ④

= 1/2
KAR

Lukuledi River

Narunyu Creek

25th Royal Fusiliers position

= 3/2
KAR ⑪

⑩

⑤

⑦

KAR
firing line

③

⑥

⑫

Narunyu

= KRAUT

② ⑧

⑭

Tapga

– 19. FK

– 4. SchK

⑨ 9. FK

⑬ 3. FK

– 11. FK

British movements
German movements
Light railway line
Newly cut road in bush
Sisal plantation
Scrub bush
Elephant grass
Swamp/marsh

N

500yd
500m

0

INTO COMBAT

Taylor's column started out before dawn on 18 August. The column marched in the following order: A Company, 1/2nd KAR (advance guard); B Company, 1/2nd KAR with four machine guns; C Company, 1/2nd KAR with four machine guns; D Company, 1/2nd KAR (minus one platoon); first-line transport (African carriers); one platoon of D Company, 1/2nd KAR; the Stokes mortars; and 25th Royal Fusiliers at the rear. The column moved on a compass bearing of 262 degrees magnetic (or 257 degrees true) for 2,500 paces; approximately 2,085yd. (The correction from magnetic bearing to true bearing in the Lindi area was approximately 5 degrees, so that degrees true equal degrees magnetic minus 5 degrees.) After a brief rest, the course was changed to 180 degrees magnetic (175 degrees true) to approach Narunyu from the north.

Progress was slowed by the dense bush and the need to proceed with caution. In the bush, both visibility and communications were greatly restricted. This could lead to suddenly and unexpectedly meeting a German unit, either one in a prepared ambush or as the result of a collision of two marching columns. Capt Angus Buchanan of 25th Royal Fusiliers later wrote of the fighting in the Lindi area:

> One had here a striking example of the difficulties of bush operations; of the disappointments, of the almost impossible task of keeping in touch with each force, across wide areas of dense, untouched, unfamiliar bush miles ahead of base. One never knows, at the commencement of a day, the full difficulties to overcome; one can never altogether foresee the obstacles that will be encountered to enforce delay, be it an impassable swamp, impenetrable forest, unbridged river, a loss of direction, or an unknown enemy force. (Buchanan (n.d.): 184)

At about 0930hrs Taylor's column discovered a newly cut road running through the bush and encountered and drove off a piquet from Abt Rothe. Detaching a patrol to follow the piquet, 1/2nd KAR deployed into bush formation astride the road and continued to advance. Because the bush was extremely dense on both sides of the road, 1/2nd KAR found that its forward progress was next to impossible and so the battalion reverted to march order at about 1200hrs. 1/2nd KAR continued to advance cautiously along the road, enduring sniper fire coming from the cover of several African huts.

Pushing onwards, the advance of 1/2nd KAR reached the top of the slope overlooking the Lukuledi River bottom lands at about 1300hrs. At this point, the Germans' fire intensified. In response, Lt-Col George Giffard, commanding 1/2nd KAR, deployed A Company in a firing line, supported it with B Company and two machine guns and then sent them forward against the Germans. As German fire was coming from the right (west), a platoon of C Company was sent forward to hold the edge of the African huts. These movements hit the boundary between Abt Rothe's 19. FK and 'Tanga' Kompagnie, and drove a wedge between these two companies. German troops were now firing from both the left and the right of 1/2nd KAR's line of advance, and soon firing began all along the line.

Between 1330hrs and 1400hrs a German force tried to flank A Company to its left (east). This force ran into B Company and its supporting machine guns and was quickly driven back. As German troops tried to move to the north against the platoon of C Company on the right, Giffard responded to this threat by sending the remainder of C Company forward to reinforce the firing line at about 1400hrs. German reinforcements – believed to have been 4. SchK – soon arrived and launched an attack on C Company from the right (west) in an attempt to outflank the line. A former German askari, Mzee Ali, described an earlier attack, thereby revealing what an 'arrow on a map' looks like to the men carrying out the attack:

> We were ordered to advance in twos and threes, so as to make it more difficult for the enemy to shoot us … The commander, another European and five askaris made the first dash. Instantly the machine gun on the hill sprang to life, emitting a volley of bullets directly on the charging men. They ran as though the devil himself were chasing them, the odds against them were too high and directly a bullet ripped through one of the askari's legs ... Five or six strides further the commander reeled back as though he'd met with some invisible wall. He staggered, trying in vain to regain his balance, but another volley of bullets laid him in the dust, the sand darkening under him. Then another askari was hit, the bullets tearing his chest apart.
>
> As I left the safety of my cover, running, doubled over, all sense of reality left me and I found myself being carried forward by some unknown force. I was aware of each individual passing moment as if the seconds had been separated from one another. Bullets were tearing up the ground in front of and behind me, ripping through the body of the man in front of me. I leapt over his fallen form and bullets cracked through the air to my left and right. I felt I would be hit at any moment. Four of us made it across ... (Quoted in MacDonell 2013: 140)

In response to the German attacks, D Company, 1/2nd KAR was brought up to extend the line to C Company's right, and its arrival helped to stop the German attack. Shortly thereafter, B Company was pulled back as battalion reserve. Firing continued as the afternoon progressed and more German reinforcements arrived and were fed into the action. At about 1500hrs Wahle added his last reserve company, 9. FK, to the fight against Taylor's column. During the fighting, German machine guns were assessed to have caused more losses than rifle fire. British commanders attributed the effectiveness of the German machine guns to their having been better directed.

While Giffard's 1/2nd KAR fought it out with Germans on the ground above Narunyu, the rest of Taylor's column closed up. At about 1700hrs No. 4 Company, 3/2nd KAR joined 1/2nd KAR in its position. (1/2nd KAR was the 'regular' 2nd Battalion of the King's African Rifles and used lettered companies, whereas 2/2nd KAR and 3/2nd KAR were wartime expansion battalions and numbered their companies 1–4.) An all-round defensive

This photograph is captioned 'Scouts cautiously feeling for the enemy through the trackless and impenetrable jungles of East Africa'. These troops were probably from 2nd Battalion, The Loyal North Lancashire Regiment which, after participating in the failed attack on Tanga in November 1914, was stationed in British East Africa. Patrolling was critical in bush warfare to provide information regarding the enemy's positions and strength, the local terrain, and the locations and capacity of water supplies. European infantry units were quickly decimated by diseases and their men lacked the bush craft needed for effective patrolling and scouting in East Africa. Both the King's African Rifles and the Schutztruppe had men with the skills and knowledge required to operate effectively in the bush. In 1914–16 King's African Rifles companies were often attached to larger British units to provide an effective reconnaissance component that was otherwise lacking. (Photo by The Print Collector/Print Collector/Getty Images)

1/2nd KAR and Abt Rothe at Narunyu

1/2nd KAR have pulled back to a defensive position. The men of Abt Rothe plus reinforcements have followed up the retirement and are attacking in an attempt to destroy the surrounded troops. A King's African Rifles Lewis-gun team and several riflemen are in shallow defensive positions – essentially scraped-out depressions with loose dirt and cut bush thrown up as a low berm to provide some cover for troops lying prone. In preparing the position, British troops had partially cleared the bush immediately around it, but beyond this the terrain remained thick with bush that provides cover to the enemy. The askari riflemen use the berm to support their SMLE rifles in the prone firing positions.

The Lewis gun, ready to be fired by the team's No. 1, is also supported on the berm with its bipod folded. The Lewis team's No. 2 is holding a spare drum magazine, ready to replace the magazine in use when it is emptied. The Lewis team's No. 3 and No. 4 have spare drum magazines to their front and sides on the ground, the magazines being within easy reach so that they can be readily handed to the No. 2 who can then hand an empty magazine back to be reloaded. Previous attacks have been repulsed with heavy firing; now the King's African Rifles askaris are now engaged in a long-range firefight with the Schutztruppe firing line that is deployed in the distant tree line.

perimeter was established 600yd behind 1/2nd KAR's firing line by the rest of the column, including the Stokes mortars and 25th Royal Fusiliers, the latter having been reduced by sickness to little more than a company – albeit one with heavy firepower in the form of four machine guns and eight Lewis guns. The decision to form this position was later viewed as a wise precaution by an officer in 25th Royal Fusiliers, since an attack could come out of the thick bush from any direction. At 1800hrs 1/2nd KAR and the attached company of 3/2nd KAR fell back to this defensive position.

Lettow-Vorbeck was now on the scene and at 1815hrs directed a fresh attack utilizing the pre-war veterans of 3. FK and 11. FK, two companies he had brought from Kilwa. This attack was intended to envelop the British right flank, but it failed to be the decisive action Lettow-Vorbeck had intended:

A Schutztruppe camouflaged observation post. A position like this would be used to conceal a sniper such as those encountered by 1/2nd KAR during its advance along the Germans' newly cut road on the ground above Narunyu. (© BArch, Bild 105-DOA3111 / Walther Dobbertin)

> Our attempt ... however only served to press it back; the bush was too thick for an offensive movement that had to be developed at short range under a continuous machine gun and rifle fire. The darkness made it still more difficult to direct the operations, and there is no doubt that in the confusion of the two fronts in this broken country our detachments often fired on one another: it was almost impossible to recognize friend and foe. (Lettow-Vorbeck (n.d.): 205)

From his perspective as a defender, Capt Buchanan of 25th Royal Fusiliers felt that these attacks appeared more threatening. He later described the fighting by alluding to past battles in which the hallowed 'infantry square' was frequently employed:

> ... for no sooner were our lines on all sides established than the enemy opened a determined attack on our right flank; and as the fight continued, fierce and sustained

attacks developed later, even in our rear and on our left. In other words the enemy were all around us and trying to break through our 'square' in the bush. It was a day of tremendous battle. There were within the circle, the first–second King's African Rifles, 25th Royal Fusiliers, and Stokes Guns, and back to back they fought, without one minute's cease in the deafening fusillade, until long after dark. (Buchanan (n.d.): 193)

The British troops within the perimeter were deployed with 25th Royal Fusiliers and D Company, 1/2nd KAR holding the western face; A and B companies, 1/2nd KAR and the attached company of 3/2nd KAR held the rest of the perimeter while C Company, 1/2nd KAR and four machine guns were held in reserve. Most of the British force within the 'square' was made up of men of 2nd King's African Rifles. There were 600-plus rifles of 2nd King's African Rifles and fewer than 160 rifles of 25th Royal Fusiliers in the perimeter. Surrounded and under fierce attack, the Fusiliers were aware that their fate depended upon the fighting qualities of their King's African Rifles compatriots. Buchanan testified to these qualities in his memoirs:

> It was here that one saw, and realized the full fighting courage to which well-trained native African troops can rise. The first–second King's African Rifles was one of the original prewar regular battalions, and magnificently they fought here; and we, who were an Imperial unit felt that we could not have wished for a stouter, nor more faithful, regiment to fight alongside of. (Buchanan (n.d.): 193)

This accolade is especially significant when one notes that 1/2nd KAR was not actually a pre-war regular battalion. 2nd Battalion, KAR, which had been disbanded by the Colonial Office in 1911 as an economy measure, had been re-formed on 1 April 1916 in Nairobi. In May 1917, 1/2nd KAR had gone into action against German forces at Schaeffer's Farm near Lindi and had been driven back by a bayonet charge when some of the new recruits panicked, resulting in a rout. Now, after hard training, frequent skirmishes, several fights, and under the leadership of one of the best officers and bush fighters in the King's African Rifles, Lt-Col George Giffard, 1/2nd KAR was proving itself a tough opponent against the veteran Schutztruppe.

An early-war photograph of a Schutztruppe unit advancing across open grass-covered ground during an exercise. The bush country in which the actions in 1917–18 were fought resulted in askaris and officers having a very limited field of view, with the result that an ordered formation such as this one could not be maintained. Under machine-gun fire, an attack quickly came to a halt as soldiers assumed prone firing positions to protect themselves from enemy fire. Unless one side could close an enemy position unseen, charges were suicidal.
(© BArch, Bild 105-DOA5011 / Walther Dobbertin)

Germans manning a Maxim MG 08 machine gun in a posed photograph from early in the war. In the bush the machine gun's position would be hidden from enemy view as much as possible, and the observer would not be sitting in plain view. German machine guns were considered by the historian of 1/2nd KAR to have caused the majority of casualties at Narunyu. (© BArch, Bild 105-DOA4018 / Walther Dobbertin)

Fighting continued until roughly 2000hrs when the German fire ceased. This quiet lasted until between 2100hrs and 2200hrs, at which time the Germans opened up with heavy fire after bugles were blown from positions 60–70yd outside the perimeters. To the British, this appeared to be a renewed attack. In the words of 1/2nd KAR's historian, 'a general, heavy attack seemed imminent. Heavy fire was returned by the companies in the perimeter together with machines guns and Stokes Guns, which lasted about 20 minutes when the enemy retired with signs of having suffered very heavily' (TNA WO 161/75).

The firing actually appears to have been cover for the German withdrawal from the immediate vicinity of the British position. Part of the German force pulled back to Narunyu and one group set up a defensive position 550yd to the north-west. After the war Lettow-Vorbeck remarked on the failure to inflict a major defeat on Linforce: 'The complete victory desired had not been attained and, in view of the difficulties of the ground, could not be expected, as we had discovered our strength to the enemy in the fighting of the 18th, and had lost the advantage of a surprise. Once more I had to content myself with delay' (Lettow-Vorbeck (n.d.): 205).

On 18 August the British suffered 33 killed and 88 wounded, with 1/2nd KAR having 12 killed (one British medical officer, one British NCO and ten Africans) and 47 wounded (two British officers, one British NCO and 44 Africans). 3/2nd KAR had ten killed (one British officer and nine Africans) and 37 wounded (three British officers, three British NCOs and 31 Africans), while 25th Royal Fusiliers suffered one killed and three wounded. The Germans suffered eight killed (six askaris and two carriers), 58 wounded (three Germans, 49 askaris and six carriers) and nine missing (six askaris and three carriers).

The fighting on 18 August indicated an increase in German strength opposing Linforce. British Intelligence reported that Lettow-Vorbeck, with half of his reserve companies, had been detected by scouts moving towards Lindi a few days before. The British responded by shifting to the defence. Based on the fighting at Narunyu, van Deventer decided not to continue Linforce's offensive. Instead, he directed that patrolling and preparations for a new attack be carried out until the British force advancing from Kilwa was ready to resume its offensive. With Linforce now digging in and awaiting help from British forces to the north, Lettow-Vorbeck had succeeded in achieving his delay.

Nyangao/Mahiwa

16–18 October 1917

BACKGROUND TO BATTLE

In mid-September 1917, Lt-Gen van Deventer decided that his forces at Kilwa and Lindi were ready to resume the offensive. His plan was for the Kilwa-based force to attack south and for Linforce to attack south-west, forcing the Germans into a smaller area in which they would have to stand and defend the vital food-producing lands, or retire and give them up. British and Belgian forces to the west would advance against the Schutztruppe's western forces and prevent them from joining the main German force. Although van Deventer wanted to destroy Lettow-Vorbeck's army in battle, he did not want his commanders to attack head-on. His directions were to pin the enemy in place, turn their flanks, then occupy positions in the enemy's rear that would force the Germans to attack in order to escape. He was committed to destroying the Schutztruppe, however, and would not shrink from a stand-up fight.

Schutztruppe units were generally understrength: 1 October 1917 returns show that most *Feldkompagnien* were at 50–75 per cent of their pre-war establishment, except for 9. FK which was 30 per cent over strength. In south-eastern German East Africa there were 25 companies with 501 Germans (130 on supply-line duty) and 2,645 askaris. Lettow-Vorbeck continued to seek an opportunity to attack and destroy a detached British force as he had at Narunyu and before. For this purpose he retained five companies as a mobile reserve ready to move in any direction as and when required.

The Nigerian Brigade takes a break during its march towards Mahiwa in October 1917. This is typical of the terrain above the Lukuledi River bottom lands and its tributaries, the vegetation being dry and difficult to move through. Behind the columns' vanguards are soldiers and pioneers with machetes to hack a path through the bush. Whenever a column would stop to rest, the first five minutes were spent hacking away the bush on both sides of the trail in an effort to widen it. Many of these trails would become the starting-points for motor roads used by supply trucks. (© IWM Q 15395)

The British offensive started on 19 September from Kilwa with two numbered columns (No. 1 and No. 2) composed of Indian and African troops, the Nigerian Brigade (less 3rd Nigerian) and a reserve. The advance from Kilwa moved steadily forwards as the Germans fought delaying actions. By the end of September the British estimated that the Germans were retreating to the south-west. Van Deventer reacted by ordering No. 1 and No. 2 columns to pursue the Germans while the Nigerian Brigade moved south to cut the retreat route of Abt Wahle opposing Linforce.

Linforce, now commanded by Maj-Gen Percival Beves, commenced its offensive on 24 September. Linforce was organized as follows: No. 3 Column under Brig-Gen O'Grady (1/2nd KAR, 3/2nd KAR and the Bharatpur Imperial Service Infantry half-battalion); No. 4 Column under Lt-Col Taylor (3/4th KAR, 30th Punjabis and the weak 25th Royal Fusiliers); and a reserve (3rd Nigerian and remnants of 8th South African Infantry). No. 3 Column marched south of the Lukuledi River heading for a position astride the enemy's line of communications from Mtama (German East Africa) to Narunyu. No. 4 Column demonstrated against Abt Wahle to fix it in place. German patrols observed the flanking movement and Wahle retired before O'Grady's force reached its objective.

Linforce continued its advance towards Mtama but, informed that the Nigerian Brigade was moving to join him, Beves slowed his advance for them to arrive. The Nigerian Brigade made contact with Linforce on 11 October and came under Beves' command. Beves estimated that he was opposed by eight or nine Schutztruppe companies in the area between Mtama and Mahiwa, six of which were facing No. 3 and No. 4 columns. The 'pin and flank' advance continued, No. 3 Column providing the pinning force and No. 4 Column the flanking force while the Nigerian Brigade would seize Mahiwa (in the Germans' rear) from the north. Movement started on 13 October with the objectives to be seized on 15 October.

The British estimate of enemy strength was erroneous, and by 15 October significant German reinforcements began arriving at Mahiwa. When German patrols detected that the Nigerian Brigade was moving south, Lettow-Vorbeck decided to reinforce Wahle and take command of the fighting against Linforce in person: 'the situation would give me a great opportunity if it could be used quickly and decisively. I ventured to hope that the intended decisive blow might now be struck for which I had tried twice near Lindi … The development of the situation on Wahle's front seemed favorable for this attempt' (Lettow-Vorbeck (n.d.): 209).

On 14 October Lettow-Vorbeck led 4. FK, 8. SchK (Abt Göring), 10. FK, 13. FK and 21. FK (Abt Ruckeschell) to Mnacho (German East Africa), arriving that night. There he added 14. FK, 17. FK and 3. SchK to his column. A short march away, 18. FK and 6. SchK had arrived under command of Hauptmann Franz Kohl while Major Georg Kraut had reached the Lukuledi River with 2. FK and 25. FK. Adding these 12 companies to Wahle's nine meant that 21 German companies were in position or moving up to oppose Linforce; 19 of these companies would participate in the impending battle.

The stage was now set for a battle that would be known as Nyangao to the British and Mahiwa to the Germans; the bloodiest battle of the East African campaign. Lettow-Vorbeck attempted to gain the elusive battlefield victory that he was continually seeking, while the British sought the decisive battle they hoped would destroy the Schutztruppe. The effort of the Nigerian Brigade to seize Mahiwa and cut Abt Wahle's line of communications caused the battle to take the shape that it did.

By the evening of 14 October the Nigerian Brigade reached Namupa Mission north-west of Wahle's positions. On the morning of the 15th, Linforce altered the brigade's orders. Now, one battalion (1st Nigerian) was to move in a south-easterly direction towards Nyangao village in order to flank Abt Wahle's position west of the Nyangao River. The rest of the Nigerian Brigade was to seize Mahiwa. The detached battalion was stopped by German forces halfway to Nyangao and dug in. The rest of the brigade advanced on Mahiwa. Lettow-Vorbeck was at Mahiwa and quickly ordered the troops with him to attack the approaching Nigerians. Faced with unexpectedly strong resistance, the Nigerians dug in on a hill overlooking the Mahiwa River. They were soon encircled and cut off from resupply. Heavy fighting continued around this position on the 16th and 17th as Lettow-Vorbeck directed attack after attack as he sought to destroy the Nigerians. Finally, early on 18 October, patrols reported an opening in the German lines to the south-east of the perimeter, and the Nigerian Brigade slipped through this gap, finally making contact with Linforce's main body.

The actions of the King's African Rifles in the battle of Nyangao/Mahiwa were part of an interrelated set of four separate fights that took place between the Nyangao River (and village) on the east, the Mahiwa River to the west, the Lukuledi River to the south and Namupa Mission to the north. This was an area of approximately 8 square miles, although the actual fighting was concentrated in several smaller locations.

The Kashmir Mountain Battery (part of the Rajah of Kashmir's Army and not a unit of the British Indian Army) going into position at Nyangao. The sterling performance of Kashmiri infantry earlier in the campaign led the British to request the battery's services for the 1917 campaign. This battery performed outstanding service in Linforce. Frequently, the Kashmir Mountain Battery deployed their four 2.75in mountain guns up front on the infantry firing line and aimed their fire directly against Schutztruppe machine-gun positions. (© IWM Q 15458)

MAP KEY

1 1500hrs, 16 October: 3/4th KAR attacks 'O' Kompagnie, 19. FK and 20. FK.

2 c.1600hrs, 16 October: Schutztruppe counter-attack drives 3/4th KAR back.

3 0815hrs, 17 October: No. 3 Column marches north-west then south-west cross-country.

4 1030hrs, 17 October: 3/4th KAR attacks Schutztruppe position west of the Nakadi River.

5 1100hrs, 17 October: No. 3 Column encounters Abt Lieberman and deploys a firing line.

6 1300hrs, 17 October: 9. FK is sent to reinforce Lieberman.

7 1400hrs, 17 October: 9. FK attacks the flank of 1/2nd KAR. C and D companies, 1/2nd KAR counter-charge, stopping the attack.

8 1500hrs, 17 October: 18. FK and 'Tanga' Kompagnie attack No. 3 Column's southern flank.

9 c.1515hrs, 17 October: 3/2nd KAR counter-attacks and restores the position.

10 1530hrs, 17 October: 3/4th KAR and 30th Punjabis attack Abt Krüger.

11 c.1540hrs, 17 October: Counter-attack by 8. SchK (plus parts of 19. FK and 'O' Kompagnie) results in a stalemate.

12 0700hrs, 18 October: 30th Punjabis and 3/4th KAR seize a foothold west of the Nakadi River.

13 0800hrs, 18 October: 18. FK moves into the gap between Abt Lieberman and Abt Krüger.

14 0830hrs, 18 October: 3/2nd KAR attacks Lieberman.

15 c.0845hrs, 18 October: 25th Royal Fusiliers is attacked in the flank by 18. FK.

16 c.0900hrs, 18 October: 1/2nd KAR charges and restores the situation.

17 1000hrs, 18 October: 10. FK and 4. SchK reinforce Abt Lieberman.

18 1100hrs, 18 October: Upon learning that the Nigerians have escaped encirclement, British attacks cease and units fall back to defensive positions.

Battlefield environment

In 1917, the countryside immediately around Nyangao and Mahiwa and along the connecting road was open and grassy; and the thinness of the vegetation made concealment difficult. These conditions were especially evident in No. 4 Column's actions along the road to Mahiwa. Since the British were on the attack, they had to cross open and grassy ground and then climb a slope to close with the enemy west of the Nakadi River.

North of the Lukuledi River, No. 3 Column fought where the vegetation was significantly denser and consisted of scrub bush, patches of elephant grass and a few scattered trees. No. 3 Column was forced to march cross-country using compass bearings in an attempt to flank the enemy. Once again, terrain and vegetation slowed movement, restricted visibility and resulted in the British advancing into the midst of Abt Lieberman's defence line.

The battlefield was extremely dry. Vegetation, especially elephant grass, was like kindling waiting for a spark or smouldering cartridge to ignite it. Once a fire started, if was not immediately extinguished, it quickly grew into a bush fire. Numbers of wounded, too injured to escape, were engulfed by the flames.

A European and askaris in trenches overlooking lower ground. Abt Wahle's askaris overlooking the dry bed of the Nakadi River would have had a similar field of fire against 3/4th KAR and 30th Punjabis on 17 and 18 October. The advantage offered by defending on higher ground helps one understand how the outnumbered Schutztruppe successfully held British attacks at bay for over two days. (Photo by ullstein bild/ullstein bild via Getty Images)

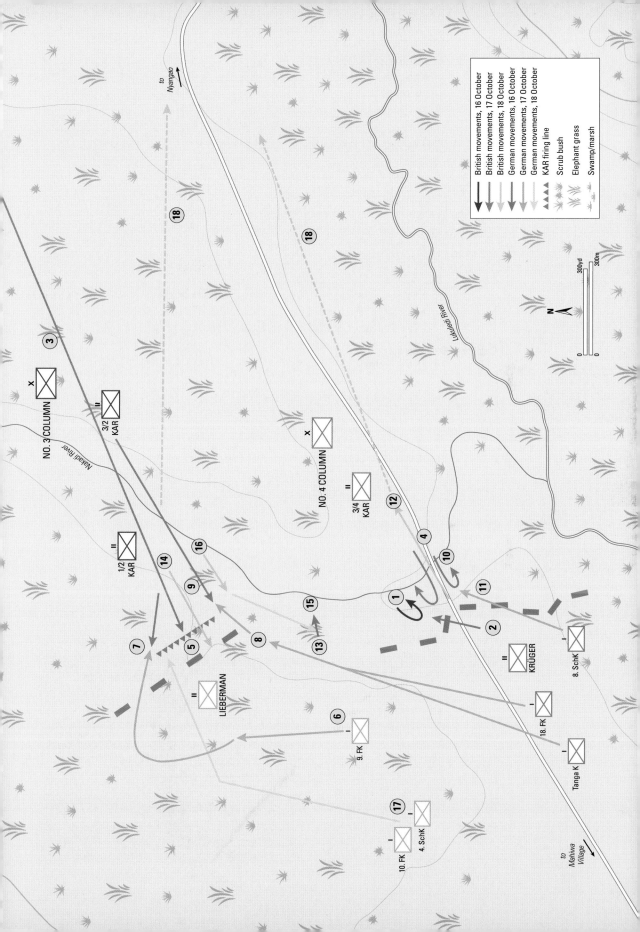

to
Nyangao

Legend:
- British movements, 16 October
- British movements, 17 October
- British movements, 18 October
- German movements, 16 October
- German movements, 17 October
- German movements, 18 October
- KAR firing line
- Scrub bush
- Elephant grass
- Swamp/marsh

N

300yd
300m
0
0

Lukuledi River

③

NO. 3 COLUMN
x

II
3/2
KAR

Nkadi River

II
1/2
KAR

⑱

⑱

④

x
NO. 4 COLUMN

II
3/4
KAR

⑫

⑭

⑯

⑨

⑩

⑮

①

⑪

②

⑧

⑤

⑦

II
LIEBERMAN

⑬

II
KRÜGER

I
8. SchK

I
18. FK

⑥

I
9. FK

I
Tanga K

⑰

I
10. FK

I
4. SchK

to
Mahiwa
Village

INTO COMBAT

Linforce's No. 3 and No. 4 columns met east of Mtama late in the afternoon of 14 October. The attempt to trap Abt Wahle failed when German patrols spotted the British columns and Wahle pulled back his troops. While the columns rested for the night, Beves received an urgent order from van Deventer early on the morning of 15 October to push on harder: 'Chief wishes you to push on now as fast as possible towards Massassi [in German East Africa, south-west of Mahiwa]. Give enemy no time to make defensive positions and make every endeavour to capture his guns. Enemy is now much shaken, and a determined advance on your line combined with operations outlined in my 549 will probably have decisive effect' (TNA CAB 44/10). The columns duly moved forwards during 15 October; but their progress was slowed by enemy delaying parties and Mtama was not reached until 1600hrs, when the British bivouacked for the night.

Despite van Deventer's assertion, the Schutztruppe veterans were not 'much shaken' and instead were ready to fight. On the morning of 16 October, Wahle's force was deployed as follows: 9. FK and 4. SchK were fighting the Nigerian Brigade near Mahiwa; 'Tanga' Kompagnie was in position south of the Lukuledi River protecting the southern flank; 'O' Kompagnie, 20. FK and 19. FK were holding a position on the west side of the Nakadi River (the main line of resistance between Mahiwa and Nyangao); and 'S' Kompagnie, 3. FK and 14. RK (Abt Lieberman) were in reserve.

Linforce's advance resumed on 16 October and just before noon No. 3 Column reached Nyangao having encountered only limited sniping. O'Grady had expected to find 1st Nigerian there and not finding the battalion was the first sign that all was not going as planned. Heavy firing could be heard in the distance to the west, indicating that the Nigerian Brigade's main body was in combat. At 1215hrs O'Grady received a message from Beves stating that three enemy companies were west of Nyangao and directing him to decide whether he should attack or wait for No. 4 Column. Beves turned command of both columns over to O'Grady who promptly, and no doubt gladly, took charge for the duration of the action.

Once No. 4 Column was up, O'Grady ordered it forwards along the road to Mahiwa and directed it to locate the German defences. No. 3 Column was to move against the northern flank of any enemy position. Moving from Nyangao at 1500hrs, 3/4th KAR led No. 4 Column towards the Nakadi River, clearing German outposts from the east side. Upon reaching the dry bed of the Nakadi, 3/4th KAR crossed it and ran into the German main position from where determined resistance was offered by the 17 Europeans and 218 askaris (with six machine guns) of 'O' Kompagnie, 19. FK and 20. FK. A sudden and violent German counter-attack by 'O' Kompagnie and 20. FK forced the KAR soldiers back to the eastern side. There they stood and stopped the Germans with support from the Kashmir Mountain Battery. With night approaching, 3/4th KAR dug in while exchanging fire with the enemy.

Late on 16 October, Beves learned that the Nigerians were encircled north of Mahiwa. In response he sent O'Grady the following message during the night of 16/17 October: 'Linforce to Colthre – Colfor supported by Colthre will attack enemy on right bank of Nyangao river at dawn 17th and drive them back …' (TNA CAB 44/10). In fact, the Nyangao River was not the

enemy's position: it was the Nakadi River, west of the Nyangao, which marked Abt Wahle's location.

Brig-Gen O'Grady planned his attack for the 17th to envelop the enemy and strike their flank while a frontal attack would keep them pinned in place. No. 4 Column (with 3/4th KAR) would provide the fixing force and, if the Germans stood their ground, No. 3 Column (with 1/ and 3/2nd KAR) would strike them from their northern flank. O'Grady knew the Nigerians at Mahiwa were in dire straits and that Linforce had to break through the enemy's defences and relieve them. Despite the return of 4. SchK from Mahiwa, Abt Wahle was reduced to six companies by the amalgamation (due to losses) of 20. FK into 'O' Kompagnie, and 'S' Kompagnie into 4. SchK; these four companies' combined strength on 15 October was 22 Germans and 255 askaris. Wahle deployed 'Tanga' Kompagnie south of the Lukuledi River to protect his right flank, 19. FK and 'O' Kompagnie (Abt Krüger) along the Nakadi River facing east, and 3. FK, 14. RK and 4. SchK (Abt Lieberman) extending the line and facing north-east in anticipation of a possible flank attack. Wahle faced the combined force of No. 3 and No. 4 columns with fewer than 600 riflemen and machine-gunners.

A staged photograph of Schutztruppe askaris firing among palms and bush. Short ranges characterized most firefights in East Africa. When two sides met in combat it was next to impossible for commanders to get a good view of the battle. One's own troops soon disappeared from view in the bush and the enemy was frequently invisible from all but the closest distance. Some participants claimed that bush fighting had more in common with night fighting than it had with fighting on the Western Front. (© BArch, Bild 105-DOA7363 / Dobbertin, Walther I 1914/1918 ca.)

3/4th KAR attacks Abt Krüger at Nyangao/Mahiwa

British view: From 3/4th KAR's perspective, the centre of an advancing platoon is shown as its European officer leads the advance. The active personal leadership displayed by British officers and NCOs leading the King's African Rifles in combat is reflected in the high rate of casualties they suffered, especially in attacks. It was not uncommon for King's African Rifles platoons and companies to lose their British leaders to enemy fire early in an action and for command to devolve onto senior indigenous NCOs. The King's African Rifles personnel are advancing without bayonets fixed to their SMLE rifles. A Lewis gun is up front with this platoon to provide automatic firepower at the point of contact. The gunner is carrying the Lewis gun such that he is ready to begin firing from the advance. His No. 2 is carrying extra drum magazines and a haversack, but does not carry a rifle. On the heights ahead, the Schutztruppe position can barely be discerned. In a short time, this ground will be a scene of carnage.

German view: The Schutztruppe holds the high ground west of, and overlooking, the Nakadi River with 19. FK and 'O' Kompagnie of Abt Krüger. The terrain is sloping down from the German position to the dry river bed. The section of the Schutztruppe's line we see is manned by 'O' Kompagnie, raised in 1915. Defence is based on the firepower of the German Maxim MG 08 tripod-mounted machine gun. The Maxim crew is commanded by a European with a European gunner, while the remaining crew, such as the ammunition-belt handler, are askaris. The askari riflemen, armed with Mauser 98s, are entrenched behind a parapet of dug-up soil, large rocks and tree trunks protecting the troops. They hold their rifles at the ready to start firing. The Schutztruppe intends to stop the British with firepower and so their bayonets are not fixed at this stage. In front of these troops the ground is more open than usual for the East African bush. 3/4th KAR can be discerned in the distance as the British advance to attack and secure this high ground breaks cover.

No. 4 Column attacked across the dry Nakadi River at 1030hrs. 3/4th KAR led the attack, supported by the Kashmir Mountain Battery (four 2.75in mountain guns) and the column's Stokes mortar battery (four mortars). 3/4th KAR drove the Schutztruppe's outposts back and were quickly engaged by the main line of resistance occupied by 19. FK and 'O' Kompagnie. Lt-Col Taylor sent 30th Punjabis forwards to support 3/4th KAR, and by 1300hrs the latter had secured part of the ridge overlooking the Nakadi River course. Shortly thereafter, the Germans started shelling the British with a 10.5cm howitzer. The British replied with fire from a pair of 5in howitzers that had been previously dragged forward to Nyangao by large gangs of indigenous carriers. For several hours the two sides settled into a firefight, neither advancing nor retreating. Hearing the sounds of No. 3 Column engaged to the north, No. 4 Column prepared another thrust. The Kashmir Mountain Battery and the Stokes mortar battery began a bombardment of the Schutztruppe defence line. Mzee Ali, a German askari, later described the experience of being under artillery fire:

It was then that the enemy artillery, well concealed in the dead ground not far from the front lines opened up and, without warning, shells came screaming down on us, exploding right in our midst, tearing our trenches to pieces. The barrage threw up a screen of smoke, dust, rocks and stones which in turn became lethal missiles. Many were killed and many more wounded yet we still had seen no sign of the advancing enemy infantry. This above all else was so unsettling that – amidst the blood and severed limbs, the wailing and agony to which one never grows accustomed – panic whipped through the ranks. (Quoted in MacDonell 2013: 165)

After the Germans had been shelled for a short period, 3/4th KAR and 30th Punjabis advanced to attack again in order to drive the Schutztruppe from the Nakadi River defences. The same askari described the infantry attack following an artillery barrage:

We did not have to wait long – like ghosts they rose through the gloom and pall of smoke… those of us who were still capable fired as rapidly as we could at these spectres of doom. Our fire did not halt their advance as they dodged from bush to tree and back to bush, taking cover where they could and rapidly returning fire. (Quoted in MacDonell 2013: 165)

Just as the attack went forwards at 1530hrs, the Germans' counter-attack struck the front and left flank of No. 4 Column. The counter-attacking Germans appear to have included 8. SchK as well as elements of 19. FK and 'O' Kompagnie, Lettow-Vorbeck having sent 8. SchK to reinforce Wahle's force earlier that day. This attack, which for a while threatened to roll No. 4 Column back on Nyangao, was repulsed by heavy firing. Both sides now recoiled from one another and took up positions for the night.

On Linforce's left (northern) flank, O'Grady started No. 3 Column off on the road to Namupa Mission at 0815hrs on 17 October. No. 3 Column consisted of the Bharatpur Imperial Service Infantry half-battalion, 1/2nd KAR and 3/2nd KAR accompanied by a two-gun section of 27th Indian Mountain Battery and the column's Stokes mortar battery (four mortars). The column marched 1,200yd along the road and then moved off to the south-west through the bush towards the Nakadi River, the intention being to outflank the German defences. Hearing the firing from the fight involving No. 4 Column, O'Grady immediately pressed his march towards the sound of the guns. The Bharatpurs led the column through the thick bush followed in order by 1/2nd KAR and 3/2nd KAR. The 27th Indian Mountain Battery section could not keep pace with the infantry moving through the bush, and so the gunners were left behind to try to make their way forwards as best they could. Around 1100hrs the Bharatpurs ran head-on into elements of the Schutztruppe, apparently 3. FK and 14. RK. The appearance of German forces here and in strength was a surprise to the British, who were expecting to outflank the Schutztruppe's Nakadi River line. What was planned as an envelopment became instead another head-on attack against prepared positions.

As soon as he saw that the Bharatpurs had encountered serious resistance, Lt-Col Giffard sent A and B companies of his 1/2nd KAR with four machine guns forwards to the Bharatpurs' right in an attempt to continue flanking the Germans. These companies were soon engaging 3. FK. The historian of 1/2nd KAR recorded that the Schutztruppe were present in overwhelming force, whereas in fact they actually numbered no more than 30 Germans and 250 askaris at first – fewer rifles than the Bharatpurs alone. It was next to impossible for officers on either side to judge the strength of their opponents. Both sides frequently thought that small groups armed with a single machine gun were entire companies. The action became an intense and confused firefight in the bush.

Earlier in the morning Lettow-Vorbeck dispatched 6. SchK and 18. FK to reinforce Wahle, who sent the former company to the Nakadi front and kept the other in reserve near his headquarters. By 1300hrs Wahle knew his left-wing forces under Lieberman were in a serious fight. Wahle brought 9. FK from its position near Mahiwa (where it had been fighting the Nigerians on 16 October) and sent it to reinforce Lieberman's troops facing O'Grady's column. The oversized 9. FK nearly doubled the number of troops opposing No. 3 Column and brought its advance to a halt. At 1400hrs, 9. FK launched a counter-attack on the right flank of the British and forced back A and B companies, 1/2nd KAR. The men of C Company advanced with fixed bayonets, passing through their comrades, and struck the Schutztruppe head-on, stopping the attack. D Company was brought up and placed in line on the right of C Company, permitting A and B companies to reorganize and return to the fray. At 1430hrs Giffard sent a message to No. 3 Column requesting reinforcements; O'Grady responded by sending forward his last reserve, 3/2nd KAR.

With no sign of British activity south of the Lukuledi River, Wahle had ordered 'Tanga' Kompagnie to move to his command post and go into reserve with 18. FK before noon. Abt Lieberman soon reported that it was running low on ammunition and that the reinforcing 9. FK was heavily engaged, so Wahle sent 18. FK and 'Tanga' Kompagnie to join Lieberman. When these two companies arrived, at approximately 1500hrs, they launched a counter-attack against the southern flank of the Bharatpur Infantry. This attack drove back the Bharatpurs and the neighbouring A and B companies, 1/2nd KAR. The first two companies of 3/2nd KAR charged the Germans as they arrived and restored the left. With his left now restored, O'Grady personally led the remainder of 3/2nd KAR to the British right flank to extend and strengthen it. As these

movements took place, 10. FK arrived from Lettow-Vorbeck's reserve and strengthened Wahle's far left flank against the possibility that the British would attempt a wider envelopment. Moving forwards, 10. FK found and brought back one abandoned Vickers machine gun and ten cases of Stokes-mortar shells. With all of No. 3 Column now in the firing line, O'Grady had to assume a defensive posture. The troops dug in as best they could along the firing line, refusing their flanks, as did the six companies of opposing Schutztruppe, the distance between the two forces being as little as 100yd. Both sides kept up heavy firing at any sign of movement and a tactical stalemate ensued.

Throughout the day's fighting the officers of 1/2nd KAR frequently exposed themselves to hostile fire to rally their men and keep the battalion in action. The vital role that officers and BNCOs played at this stage is evident in the loss of 52 per cent of these personnel on this day of fighting alone. In addition, 54 per cent of the battalion's askaris became casualties. The machine-gun specialists suffered heavily since both sides made strenuous efforts to target them. During the fighting on 17 October, all eight machine-gun teams of 1/2nd KAR were put out of action. Later, one abandoned machine gun was observed in front of C Company's line, and believing it to be a German gun, the company charged to capture it. The askaris soon saw that the dead crewmen around the gun were their King's African Rifles comrades. After reorganizing the battered battalion during the night, Giffard was able to man only two machine guns and four Lewis guns with improvised crews; the battalion had gone into action that morning with eight of each.

During the afternoon's fighting bush fires broke out in places, the extremely dry grass being quick to ignite from sparks or any flame. The fires quickly burned away the tall elephant grass, leaving the harder scrub bushes

No. 3 Column, expecting to strike the rear of the German line along the Nakadi River, was surprised to run head-on into Abt Lieberman's defences on 17 October. Short lines of sight in the bush and the Schutztruppe's skill in preparing concealed positions resulted in the British advances coming to an abrupt halt when contact was made. The British had to determine whether the German force was only a delaying detachment or the main line of resistance, then plan an attack and deploy their column accordingly, all the while watching for a possible counter-attack to come out of the bush. (© BArch, Bild 134-C0313 / Dobbertin, Walther I 1914/1918 ca.)

scorched but standing. The scrub remained an obstacle to movement and still provided concealment for defensive positions prepared by seasoned bush fighters. Bush fires were a constant problem in the dry season and posed a deadly threat to troops that was not found on the Western Front. A Schutztruppe askari later described the terror of a bush fire:

> Strict instructions were issued regarding fires and the dangers of starting a grass fire out of carelessness. A fire, out of control, would destroy all our ammunition and equipment … the fire seemed to leap-frog ahead of itself, consuming itself as it spread. This effect brought in our first casualties, encircling and trapping men in the flames … Not only were we trying to escape death but so too were many of the animals in the surrounding bush … Indeed there is nothing more frightening than witnessing by the light of flames, cobras and other snakes moving towards you at great speed with their upper bodies raised. The only thing to do is stand perfectly still. Their fear has primed them to strike at any obstacle in their path, thus you should not present yourself as one. But many of the porters lacked the courage to keep still as a six-foot cobra hurtled towards them, a foot of its body in the air, its hood fanning out on either side. And they just kept coming, dozens of them pouring out of the grass. (Quoted in MacDonell 2013: 161)

During the night of 17/18 October both sides adjusted their positions, sometimes causing the enemy to let off bursts of fire. German forces were rearranged such that 10. FK, 13. FK and 8. SchK returned to Lettow-Vorbeck's reserve, while 6. SchK and 18. FK remained with Wahle. O'Grady remained in command of the two British columns and at 2000hrs issued instructions to Taylor for a renewed effort the next day: 'It is of the utmost importance that you should throw your whole weight against the enemy still opposed to you. The two Nigerian battalions at Mahiwa have not had food for two days and must be extricated. An exceptional effort is required on your part, and this should commence at dawn' (TNA CAB 44/10).

Early on 18 October patrols were pushed forwards by Linforce. On No. 4 Column's front these patrols reported that there was no sign of the Germans. No. 3 Column's patrols found the enemy firmly in place, however, and showing no signs of withdrawing. Abt Wahle was still manning its defences: Abt Krüger (19. FK and 'O' Kompagnie, apparently with 6. SchK which had been added during the fighting on the 17th) faced No. 4 Column; Abt Lieberman (3. FK, 14. RK and 4. SchK) was opposite No. 3 Column; and 9. FK, 18. FK and 'Tanga' Kompagnie were held in reserve. A gap of approximately 500–600yd separated both the two German *Abteilungen* and the two British columns.

No. 4 Column started its attack at 0700hrs with 30th Punjabis while sending the remnants of 25th Royal Fusiliers (126 strong) to extend the right flank to the north and try to close the gap between it and No. 3 Column. The attack immediately ran into heavy resistance and the Fusiliers lost their direction in the bush. The Punjabis pushed ahead, seizing the high ground west of the Nakadi River bed and then digging in to hold against the expected German counter-attack. 3/4th KAR advanced on the left (southern) flank of the Punjabis and also took ground west of the Nakadi and dug in. Both battalions were now engaged in a heavy firefight with Abt Krüger, and No. 4 Column was unable to advance any further. At about 1100hrs, 6. SchK counter-attacked the Punjabis and drove them back across the Nakadi, which in turn forced 3/4th KAR to retreat. With the dry river bed separating the opponents, the fighting in this sector became stalemated while the troops continued to exchange heavy fire.

On No. 3 Column's front, O'Grady ordered 3rd Nigerian to undertake a movement to link up with its sister battalions trapped near Mahiwa and help them to reach Linforce's main body. This battalion would take a route well north of Wahle's positions in the hope of bypassing German resistance. No. 3 Column itself would attack Abt Lieberman's position in an attempt to smash through the defences. While conducting a personal and risky reconnaissance of his front, O'Grady met the lost 25th Royal Fusiliers of No. 4 Column; he decided to use these troops to attack the northern flank of the Germans opposing No. 4 Column by driving southwards through the gap between Abt Krüger and Abt Lieberman. He planned to support the Fusiliers by having his left-flank battalion, 3/2nd KAR, attack the enemy directly in front

of them. At 0830hrs the King's African Rifles soldiers launched their attack and were immediately countered by heavy enemy machine-gun fire. The leading troops advanced roughly 200yd before being driven to the ground by a heavy crossfire from their immediate front and their right (northern) flank. Now the Fusiliers charged to the attack; but they had mistakenly moved north instead of south, and disaster struck. Shortly before this attack, Wahle had positioned 18. FK from his reserve into the gap; and the Fusiliers, who moved across the German front, suffered heavily from effective enfilade machine-gun fire followed by a Schutztruppe bayonet charge.

The Germans, emboldened by the losses suffered by the Fusiliers, swept forwards into the left flank of No. 3 Column, threatening to envelope 3/2nd KAR. B and D companies, 1/2nd KAR (now with a combined strength of 120 men) were moving up to extend the left flank as the Germans approached. Immediately, D Company deployed in the firing line, with C Company initially in reserve for a short period until it too was deployed to help hold the line. The column's section of 27th Mountain Battery provided fire support to the defenders and a heavy firefight began. The German askaris' advance was stopped, and another stalemate ensued in the bush. Neither side could accurately gauge the strength of their opponent. The Germans brought up 10. FK from Lettow-Vorbeck's main reserve and this company, with 4. SchK, launched a fresh wave of attacks on the British firing line. These attacks were

11th (Hull) Heavy Battery, Royal Garrison Artillery, brought two 5.4in howitzers into battle at Nyangao/Mahiwa. Pulled to the front by immense indigenous labour gangs, these guns came as an unwelcome surprise to the Germans. They replied to the German artillery fire and shelled Abt Wahle's position in preparation for the attack of 3/4th KAR. Unfortunately for the British, the howitzers had a limited supply of shells: their weight made resupply by indigenous carriers difficult. (© IWM Q 15508)

King's African Rifles troops in a defensive position. Following Brig-Gen Henry de Courcy O'Grady's orders to break contact and pull back to defensive positions, Linforce's No. 3 and No. 4 columns withdrew to the open ground around Nyangao and dug in to prepare for a possible Schutztruppe counter-attack. Field positions, similar to those illustrated here, were set up and the two columns linked their positions together. No attack came, however, as both sides had suffered heavy losses and the Germans needed to sort out their jumbled companies, collect abandoned British equipment and shift their white command cadre around to replace leadership casualties. (© IWM Q 15387)

repulsed without any special mention of their occurrence on the part of No. 3 Column. Around 1100hrs, elements of 3rd Nigerian joined the firing line, relieving B and D companies, 1/2nd KAR, which rejoined the rest of their battalion in reserve.

3rd Nigerian brought news that the other Nigerians had escaped their encirclement near Mahiwa and that the attacks were no longer needed. No. 4 Column withdrew to the east bank of the Nakadi River, which increased the gap separating the two columns. In expectation of further German attacks, O'Grady pulled No. 3 Column back to a more defensible position for the night and linked up with No. 4 Column. The historian of 1/2nd KAR summed up the fighting as follows: 'Both the Germans and ourselves fought each other to a complete standstill, and it was utterly impossible for us to think of a further advance after this action until the force was reorganized and supplies and ammunitions brought up' (TNA WO 161/75).

With Linforce's withdrawal the Germans could claim a victory, but it was a costly triumph: their strength was placed by the British official historian at roughly 1,500 rifles; their losses were 99 killed, six missing and 420 wounded. The British fighting strength was approximately 4,500 rifles (including Lewis-gun and machine-gun crews); losses amounted to 383 killed and missing, and 1,072 wounded. Together, 1/and 3/2nd KAR lost 62 killed and 254 wounded. The two battalions, understrength at the start of the battle, were temporarily consolidated into a composite unit until replacements could arrive. British losses could be made good, but German losses – especially among the European officers and other ranks – were irreplaceable.

Lioma

30–31 August 1918

BACKGROUND TO BATTLE

German losses during the 1917 dry-season fighting had been heavy. The mobile defence of German East Africa had delayed its conquest but now – with the Germans cut off from outside support, running low on ammunition, short on the quinine needed by the Europeans to counter malaria, and trying to hold onto their last food-growing areas – many on both sides expected a German surrender. That was not an option to Lettow-Vorbeck, however, who decided instead to adopt a new strategy:

> Our large force with little ammunition was of less value in the field than a smaller number of picked men with plenty of ammunition. It amounted to a reduction of our strength to about 2,000 rifles, including not more than 200 Europeans. All above this number had to be left behind. Some of those left did not object to being out of the war … it must be admitted that among those who were left behind at Nanbindinga, even among the Europeans, there were many who were not unwilling to lay down their arms. (Lettow-Vorbeck (n.d.): 220)

The number of personnel purged from the fighting force amounted to approximately 700 Europeans and 2,000 askaris. Lettow-Vorbeck's main force was reduced to brigade size; 15 companies remained when weakened or poorly performing companies were consolidated with ones having better command cadres. Lettow-Vorbeck was counting on doubling this strength when he met up with the Schutztruppe's Westtruppen (commanded by Hauptmann Theodor Tafel) retreating towards him while pursued by British and Belgian forces. Unfortunately, Lettow-Vorbeck's force and the Westtruppen passed each other in the dense bush about 1¼ miles apart near the appointed rendezvous on 27 November. That same day, Hanforce's No. 1 Column hit the front of the Westtruppen and No. 2 Column struck its rear. On 28 November, surrounded and with no word of Lettow-Vorbeck's location, the Westtruppen surrendered to the British; 148 Europeans and roughly 1,400 askaris were taken prisoner.

In November 1917 the remaining Schutztruppe invaded Portuguese East Africa. This was not an attempt to conquer, but a foraging expedition. The German force moved constantly, searching out supplies and opportunities to defeat enemy detachments while avoiding being pinned down by superior forces. Most food supplies, especially for Africans, were foraged from the countryside through which the force marched. Successful actions against the Portuguese provided the Germans with captured arms, ammunition, medical supplies, some foodstuffs and other vitally important items. During one of the first encounters of Lettow-Vorbeck's invasion in late November 1917 he captured much-needed medical supplies, a large number of rifles, six machine guns, 250,000 rounds of ammunition and several tons of European supplies. So many Portuguese Mauser rifles (a smaller-bore version of the Mauser 98) were captured that these provided the majority of the Schutztruppe's rifles. The German commander recorded 'With one blow we had freed ourselves of a great part of our difficulties' (Lettow-Vorbeck (n.d.): 232). This action set the pattern for future encounters between the Schutztruppe and the Portuguese, with the latter becoming the unwilling quartermasters for the Schutztruppe.

Although Portugal's metropolitan forces sent several large contingents to Portuguese East Africa, they and their colonial troops proved to be of little use fighting the Schutztruppe. The British had to shoulder the burden of fighting in the Portuguese territory. In 1918 British infantry was African, primarily provided by 13 King's African Rifles battalions, the Rhodesian Native Regiment, the Northern Rhodesian Police (militarized African police) and – until June – the battalion-sized Gold Coast Regiment from West Africa. Several Indian mountain batteries provided artillery support and European personnel from Britain and South Africa fulfilled a plethora of technical duties. As always, large numbers of African carriers were required to provide transportation of supplies for the force in the field.

By August 1918, the remaining Schutztruppe were east of Lake Nyasa and heading north intent on returning to German East Africa. Lettow-Vorbeck targeted a British supply dump at Regone in Portuguese East Africa – papers captured in an encounter with part of 2/4th KAR on 24 August indicated that Regone held large stocks of supplies including 10,000 carrier-loads of food, 500 cases of small-arms ammunition, and 200 Stokes-mortar shells. The papers also showed that British columns were converging on Lettow-Vorbeck from the south, south-east and north-west. Despite the threat of encirclement, his supply needs compelled him to plan to attack Regone on 25 August, his assumption being that Regone would not be reinforced until 26 August.

A quick assault would give his troops enough time to collect as many of the pre-packaged supplies that they could carry and destroy the remainder. The Schutztruppe set out on a night march to reach its target by the early morning of 25 August, but they were delayed by rough terrain, rain and fog. When Lettow-Vorbeck eventually reached Regone, he found it had already been reinforced and fortified and was no longer vulnerable to being stormed quickly. With several British columns moving towards him, he cancelled his planned attack, and moved north, bypassing Regone and marching towards Lioma.

In the last week of August, van Deventer ordered a concentration against the Schutztruppe in the area of Regone and Lioma. On 23 August 2/4th KAR arrived at Regone and sent half of its strength to the south, where it ran into the Schutztruppe on the 24th. 3/4th KAR reached Regone while this action was under way and joined in fortifying the British positions. By 26 August 1/4th KAR and the Rhodesian Native Regiment had arrived at Regone, causing Lettow-Vorbeck to bypass that position. To the north, 2/ and 3/1st KAR and the Northern Rhodesian Police were concentrating to block an enemy advance into Nyasaland. On 28 August 1/1st KAR reached Lioma and proceeded to dig in and patrol the routes to the south by which the enemy would approach. Moving from the south-east, KARTUCOL (KAR 2nd Column, comprising 1/, 2/ and 3/2nd KAR) was force-marching, covering up to 20 miles a day, trying to reach Lioma before the Schutztruppe. If it all worked out, van Deventer would trap the German force between four battalions at Lioma and four battalions at Regone, with three more battalions in positions to join a battle.

1/1st KAR reached Lioma during the evening of 28 August. A square defensive perimeter was established about ½ mile south of the village and the troops dug in. The sides of this square measured roughly 400yd. The perimeter served to control the road along which the Germans were expected to be marching, which ran parallel to the Luala River. Three detached platoon posts were set up outside this square; one to the west and one to the south about 1,000yd away, and one east about 400yd away. After deducting two combat patrols sent out to scout for the Germans, the main position was held by 10½ platoons. On 29 August the battalion continued to prepare for the expected enemy appearance, the only action being an exchange of gunfire at the southern outpost.

While the Schutztruppe moved across Portuguese East Africa foraging and capturing supplies whenever and wherever possible, the British stayed in pursuit or tried to intercept them. Frequent fights occurred as van Deventer's columns attempted to corner the Schutztruppe and end the campaign. Despite some close calls, the Germans remained just ahead of their pursuers, or managed to fight their way out of traps. On 5 July 1918 the Schutztruppe comprised 209 Europeans and 1,257 askaris armed with 1,003 Portuguese Mausers, 166 British rifles, 65 black-powder M71 rifles, 13 German Maxim machine guns, 17 captured Vickers machine guns and nine captured Lewis guns. Schutztruppe units armed with black-powder M71 rifles gave away their positions when firing because of the clouds of smoke created by their rifles – and the smoke around M71-armed troops gave the British a point at which to direct their fire. For many German askaris the only replacement for the M71 came from capturing modern rifles from the enemy. The November 1917 reduction of the Schutztruppe by Lettow-Vorbeck allowed most of the remaining askaris to be armed with modern smokeless rifles. The remaining M71s were discarded during the campaign in Portuguese East Africa when large stocks of Portuguese Mausers and ammunition were captured. (© BArch, Bild 105-DOA7086 / Dobbertin, Walther I 1914/1918 ca.)

MAP KEY

1 **Dawn, 30 August:** 1/1st KAR is deployed ½ mile south of Lioma.

2 *c.*1200hrs, 30 August: The Schutztruppe's advance guard encounters the eastern outpost.

3 *c.*1200hrs, 30 August: 3/2nd KAR deploys 1 mile north east of Lioma.

4 **1400hrs, 30 August:** The Schutztruppe moves east and west of 1/1st KAR to attack from all sides.

5 *c.*1430hrs, 30 August: Abt Poppe overruns 1/1st KAR's southern outpost.

6 *c.*1630hrs, 30 August: Abt Müller and Abt Poppe attack the eastern and southern sides of the position.

7 *c.*1630hrs, 30 August: 3/2nd KAR captures Abt Müller's baggage and reserve ammunition.

8 *c.*1800hrs, 30 August: 3/2nd KAR attacks the Germans west of Lioma.

9 **2230hrs, 30 August:** The Germans cease their attacks and withdraw southwards.

10 **0400hrs, 31 August:** 2/2nd KAR and HQ KARTUCOL arrive east of Lioma.

11 **0900hrs, 31 August:** The Schutztruppe moves north-east, Abt Müller leading followed by Abt Göring.

12 **1000hrs, 31 August:** Germans movements sighted; 2/2nd and two companies of 3/2nd KAR move to intercept.

13 c.1200hrs, 31 August: 2/2nd KAR makes contact with the Schutztruppe.

14 c.1300hrs, 31 August: 3/2nd KAR extends the British line north.

15 c.1300hrs, 31 August: German main body continues to the north-east.

16 **1430hrs, 31 August:** 1/2nd KAR encounters the Germans and overruns a field hospital.

17 *c.*1600hrs, 31 August: The Schutztruppe breaks contact, withdrawing north-eastwards.

Battlefield environment

Lioma is located on a plateau in what is today western Mozambique. To the east and west of Lioma the land rises and tall heights overlook the village and its connecting roads. Lioma is approximately 2,000ft above sea level, with hills rising to over 4,000ft above sea level. In many places, the hills rise in steep slopes with frequent cliffs. In between the hills there are streams with rocky beds that cut deep into the surrounding terrain. Here in the highlands, the country was covered by bush interspersed with timber trees. The dense vegetation obstructed vision, impaired movement, slowed communications and constrained the ability of commanders to judge the course of an action. Neither side knew the area and had to rely on local guides (often of dubious reliability), inaccurate maps, compass bearings and landmarks to find their way through the country. Roads were little more than rough trails and basic tracks between villages; many of these had until the last two decades of the 19th century been routes used by Arab slave-hunting expeditions.

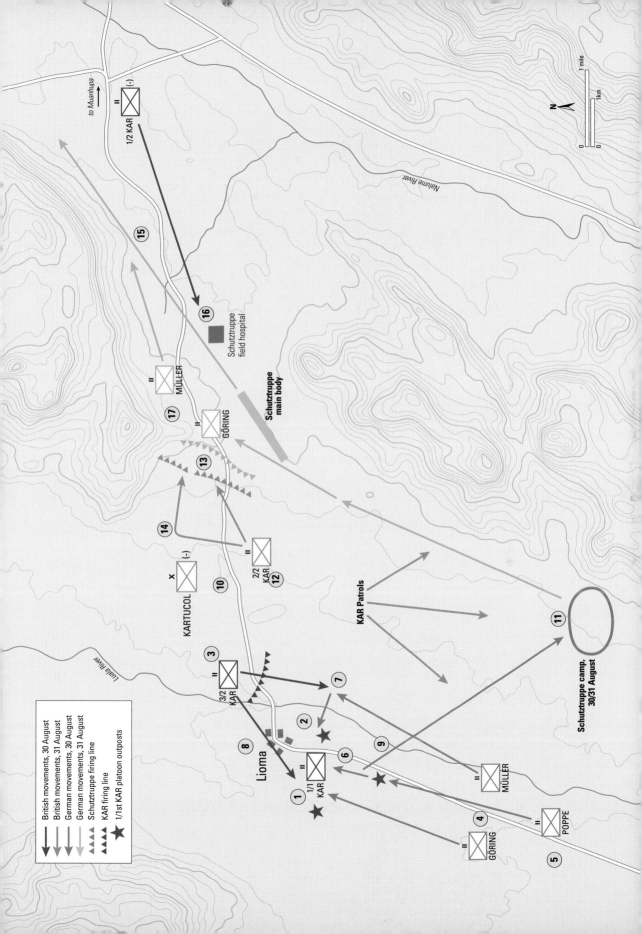

to Muanhupa

1/2 KAR II (-)

(15)

(16)

Schutztruppe field hospital

Schutztruppe main body

MÜLLER II

(17)

GÖRING II

(13)

(14)

KARTUCOL x (-)

(10)

2/2 KAR II

(12)

Nalume River

KAR Patrols

Luala River

(3)

3/2 KAR II

(7)

(2)

Lioma

(8)

1/1 KAR II

(1)

(6)

(9)

MÜLLER II

(4)

GÖRING II

POPPE II

(5)

Schutztruppe camp, 30/31 August

(11)

N

1 mile

1km

Legend:
British movements, 30 August
British movements, 31 August
German movements, 30 August
German movements, 31 August
Schutztruppe firing line
KAR firing line
1/1st KAR platoon outposts

INTO COMBAT

The 13 surviving companies of the Schutztruppe were approaching Lioma on 30 August. Exact company assignments for 30 and 31 August are not available; the estimated assignments given here are based on those listed prior to, or after, the Lioma action and the position those detachments had within the Schutztruppe organization for its marches. In the lead was Abt Müller, appearing to consist of 4. SchK, 9. FK and either 3. or 13. FK. These were the first Schutztruppe elements to make contact with 1/1st KAR south of Lioma. At about 1200hrs Müller's vanguard was sighted by 1/1st KAR's detached platoon dug in east of the main position and equipped with one Vickers machine gun and one Lewis gun. The King's African Rifles opened fire on the leading askaris. The Germans quickly returned fire and then pulled back towards Müller's main body. While this first skirmish was occurring, Lt-Col Philips' 3/2nd KAR of KARTUCOL reached Lioma. 3/2nd KAR deployed north-east of 1/1st KAR's main position, with approximately 1 mile separating the battalions.

Lettow-Vorbeck arrived on the scene and assessed that the British had just arrived and had not had time to complete digging in given the small platoon-sized outpost, but this proved to be an erroneous assumption. He ordered both Abt Müller and Abt Göring (the latter apparently comprising 3. SchK, 2. FK and either 3. or 13. FK) to march around the British position to attack it from the north. While these movements were occurring Abt Poppe, consisting of two companies (these appear to have been 6. SchK and 11. FK), assaulted 1/1st KAR's forward platoon's position around 1430hrs and overran it. Elements of D Company, 1/1st KAR went forward to support the outpost, but were only able to assist the survivors retiring to the main perimeter. Contact between the two King's African Rifles battalions was broken after 1500hrs as German forces were moving around 1/1st KAR's position, and would continue to do so during the rest of the day and the subsequent night.

Around 1630hrs the Germans began vigorously attacking the main position of 1/1st KAR. These attacks began on the eastern front of the square defensive perimeter and were followed by attacks from the north (by Abt Müller), and

A Schutztruppe column on a road march led by a senior indigenous NCO in open country. This photograph was taken either just before the war or in the early days of the conflict. The fighting between the Schutztruppe and the King's African Rifles during 1917–18 occurred in bush and forest country where few roads existed, with movement being conducted either along trails and tracks or by hacking through the bush on compass bearings. The column of twos would frequently be reduced to single file in thick bush country, causing columns to stretch out in length and thereby increasing their vulnerability to flank attacks. (© BArch, Bild 105-DOA3133 / Dobbertin, Walther I 1914/1918 ca.)

from the south (by Abt Poppe). While 1/1st KAR was being attacked, 3/2nd KAR launched counter-attacks. The first counter-attack, mounted by a company of 3/2nd KAR – the exact company designation is not recorded in the sources – against Müller's troops on the perimeter's eastern side, saw the baggage and reserve ammunition of Abt Müller captured and its carriers scattered.

Another German unit – apparently Abt Göring – moving west of 1/1st KAR's position was attacked by another company of 3/2nd KAR from the north. This attack was supported by the battalion's single Stokes mortar that was deployed north-east of Lioma. With Göring's northwards movement blocked, he deployed part of his strength to oppose 3/2nd KAR and employed the remainder to attack the western face of 1/1st KAR's perimeter, the overrunning of which was the Germans' goal. Repeated charges by the three *Abteilungen* caused 1/1st KAR's African porters to panic; many ran off into the bush, fortunately leaving the supplies and ammunition in the perimeter. 1/1st KAR's shooting was later judged to have been excellent from the number of killed and wounded left around the perimeter.

German attacks continued until 2230hrs when, with casualties mounting among irreplaceable European cadres, Göring decided that 1/1st KAR's

A King's African Rifles unit manning trenches. The dense bush would conceal the approach of the enemy until they were within close range, making it necessary to place outposts and pickets in front of a defended position to alert the main body that the enemy was approaching. This is why 1/1st KAR deployed platoon-sized outposts on the approaches to Lioma and sent out patrols to locate the Schutztruppe. Early warning was needed for the defenders to man their fighting positions and be prepared mentally to face an attack. (© IWM Q 69874)

position could not be taken by a night assault and he ordered a withdrawal. After breaking contact with the British, the German-led troops retired to the south to join the rest of the Schutztruppe. The British command believed that the Schutztruppe attack on Lioma had been an effort to cover the German movement around 1/1st KAR and escape to the north. Having held the position, and prevented the Schutztruppe's attempts to bypass it by aggressive counter-attacks, the British saw an opportunity to 'bag' the elusive Schutztruppe once and for all. On the German side Lettow-Vorbeck felt that his troops had destroyed one British force (actually only one platoon), but were still threatened by converging British columns and needed to break away from their pursuers on 31 August and gain a respite.

To the east of Lioma, 1/2nd KAR reached Muanhupa in Portuguese East Africa at 0840hrs on 30 August after a hard night march. The headquarters of KARTUCOL and 2/2nd KAR then set off to march to Lioma from Muanhupa at 1215hrs. By 2000hrs the headquarters and 2/2nd KAR crossed the Nalume River (between Lioma and Muanhupa) when word was received from 3/2nd KAR that a battle with the entire Schutztruppe was in progress at Lioma. Lt-Col Giffard ordered a halt to enable the troops and African carriers to be fed. He also sent orders to 1/2nd KAR to move to the Nalume River crossing and block a road that ran northwards through a gap in the hills by which the Germans could attempt to bypass the British around Lioma. Column headquarters and 2/2nd KAR resumed their march at midnight and reached a position 2 miles east of Lioma at 0400hrs on 31 August. Now, three King's African Rifles battalions were in the vicinity of Lioma and a fourth was located to the east within four hours' march.

After assessing the situation during the night of 30/31 August, Lettow-Vorbeck decided that his force needed to move east of Lioma to continue its march north. Having lost some ten Europeans (at least four killed and six wounded) on 30 August, Lettow-Vorbeck shuffled his remaining European leaders to fill the gaps as best as possible and redistributed the remaining stocks of ammunition. Keeping with his practice of moving in *Abteilungen*, at 0900hrs on 31 August Lettow-Vorbeck started his march north to escape the Lioma area in several columns. Once more, Hauptmann Erich Müller led the advance with Hauptmann Karl Göring close behind, Generalmajor Wahle was in charge of the main body, and Hauptmann Paul Stemmermann led the rearguard. By having Wahle direct the march of the main body, Lettow-Vorbeck was free to move through the force, checking on progress and able to respond quickly to any actions. Seriously wounded and sick Schutztruppe personnel, and sick prisoners, were left behind in the charge of a captured British medical officer to speed up the German force's movement. Now operating in an unknown country and lacking reliable guides, the Germans were forced to rely on compass bearings and landmarks, such as the hills to the east, to govern their progress. They no longer had the capability for rapid and accurate movement in the bush that had been a hallmark of their operations in German East Africa.

Early on 31 August, Giffard met Lt-Col Phillips, CO 3/2nd KAR, to obtain an understanding of the situation. Giffard was informed that the majority of the Schutztruppe had withdrawn from in front of 3/2nd KAR overnight and had moved south. 3/2nd KAR had sent out patrols but as of 0400hrs had not made contact with 1/1st KAR at Lioma, and had encountered small parties of the enemy but had not located its main body. At 0900hrs contact was finally made with 1/1st KAR and Giffard learned from that unit that a large number of enemy campfires had been seen through the night about 5 miles south of that battalion's position. At about 1000hrs a report was received from an officer's patrol watching the enemy's camp that the Schutztruppe was moving towards the north-east via a route that ran along the hills east of Lioma. This route would cross the road along which KARTUCOL's troops had marched the day and night before.

Giffard ordered 2/2nd KAR followed by half of 3/2nd KAR to move back along the road and engage the enemy moving to the north-east. The officer's patrol reported that another enemy unit of unknown size was moving westward. Since Maj Alexander Masters, CO 1/1st KAR, reported that his battalion was badly shaken from the previous day's fighting, Giffard decided to use that battalion to defend the baggage and reserve ammunition and hold the

Although staged, this photograph illustrates a dispersed and prone firing line in open terrain. The officers and NCOs standing behind the askaris would have been early casualties in a real firefight. Because opponents with modern weapons rendered the close ranks of pre-war formations obsolete, dispersal, cover and concealment became critical. It also meant fewer troops could defend longer lines. Many of the photographs of the Schutztruppe that exist today, such as this one, were taken by German photographer, and German East Africa planter, Walther Dobbertin, who recorded the war in the territory until he was captured in 1916. (BArch, Bild 105-DOA6661 / Dobbertin, Walther I 1914/1918 ca.)

other half of 3/2nd KAR back as a mobile reserve. Now knowing where the enemy force was and its direction of march, at 1100hrs Giffard used the field telephone to order 1/2nd KAR to advance and attack the enemy from the east.

2/2nd KAR, with No. 1 and No. 3 companies in the lead, struck the flank of the leading Germans as they reached the Lioma–Muanhupa road around 1200hrs. The fighting quickly developed and became a stubborn contest between the King's African Rifles, sensing the opportunity at least to damage the enemy heavily, if not to destroy him, and Abt Müller and Abt Göring, intent on survival. No. 2 and No. 4 companies, 2/2nd KAR came up and deployed south (on the right flank) of their sister companies. The German main body had been observed by patrols on the march, and their carrier column was now a prime target for the British because capturing supplies and scattering the carriers would inflict a major logistical loss on the Schutztruppe. With this in mind the half-battalion of 3/2nd KAR that was following 2/2nd KAR deployed to the left (northern) flank, extended the line and tried to overlap the head of the enemy's column so that they could attack the Schutztruppe's carriers. The Germans had already extended their line to a rugged hill to the north, however, and this position covered the movement of their carriers and non-combatants as they moved first a short distance east along the Lioma–Muanhupa road and then struck northwards along a trail.

The fighting degenerated into a stagnant firefight in the bush, with neither side able to gain an advantage. When he arrived at Abt Müller, Lettow-Vorbeck began to think of attacking. He decided the six companies of 2/2nd KAR and 3/2nd KAR were ripe for being the target of a knock-out blow against a detached British force (as had been his intention at Narunyu and Nyangao/Mahiwa as well as on many other occasions during the campaign). Lettow-Vorbeck thought that he could catch these units between his advance and his main body. Sending a messenger to bring up the rest of the Schutztruppe, he quickly surveyed the position to formulate a plan. Shortly afterwards, however, he found to his dismay that the main force had marched past his position along a track to the east and had proceeded north parallel to his advance *Abteilungen*. This error may have worked to Lettow-Vorbeck's benefit: had he massed against the six companies to his west, he would have been attacked in the rear by 1/2nd KAR advancing from the east, whose presence he was unaware of until the battalion struck Abt Stemmermann.

At 1120hrs, 1/2nd KAR started its march westwards in response to KARTUCOL's 1100hrs order. In ten minutes the battalion encountered the column's Indian field ambulance that had been left behind by the main body of KARTUCOL during its move to Lioma. D Company was deployed as a screen and advance guard as the battalion marched towards Lioma. By 1430hrs D Company encountered the enemy. Pushing the German pickets back, the battalion came under fire from snipers posted on high hills to the right (north) of the road. A complete German field hospital was overrun as the battalion advanced. When the commander of D Company was wounded, the troops turned to the right and advanced against the hills from which the enemy was firing. As the main body of the battalion arrived, the Schutztruppe began firing two machine guns from positions on the hill; but their aim was poor, with the machine-gun rounds striking 50yd in front of the troops. Nevertheless, this fire led to confusion and caused the battalion's African carriers to run.

Schutztruppe askaris on the march led by two Germans. This photograph illustrates how the askaris' dress changed during the war from traditional uniforms to whatever could be utilized. An *Abteilung* was accompanied by its carriers with reserve ammunition, medical supplies, food and camp equipment. It was only through the efforts of the carriers that the Schutztruppe remained a force to be reckoned with; but the carrier columns were vulnerable when moving in single file along bush tracks. At Lioma, the King's African Rifles were able to attack the Schutztruppe baggage on both days and scatter and capture part of their supplies. (Photo by ullstein bild/ullstein bild via Getty Images)

C Company quickly deployed on both sides of the road, with half facing north and half facing south. A Company deployed astride the road linking the two halves of C Company. Meanwhile, D Company cleared the hill it had attacked north of the road, the Schutztruppe retiring in disorder and inflicting few casualties. After 1500hrs the Schutztruppe soldiers could be seen retiring from their positions and heading north. 1/2nd KAR regrouped to continue its advance and secure the prisoners from the captured field hospital. Because B Company, assigned the previous night to block a road to the south-east, was detached from the battalion, 1/2nd KAR brought only 350 riflemen and machine-gunners to this fight. At 1600hrs the King's African Rifles advance towards Lioma was cautiously resumed as a captured Schutztruppe askari claimed that four fresh enemy companies were advancing towards 1/2nd KAR. At about 1700hrs, contact was made with patrols from both 2/2nd KAR and 3/2nd KAR, and soon three battalions of 2nd King's African Rifles reunited on the battlefield which was by now empty of German-led troops other than the dead, wounded and prisoners.

The Germans managed to escape and were able to continue their march north to return to German East Africa – but they had failed to capture Lioma and thus were not able to replenish their supplies. They had lost heavily in the fighting, especially in their command cadre, but the extent of their losses for 30/31 August varies according to different sources. Lettow-Vorbeck lists the following losses: among the Europeans, six killed, 11 wounded and five missing; among the askaris, 23 killed, 16 wounded, 29 missing and five captured (Lettow-Vorbeck (n.d.): 299). A British history of the King's African Rifles lists German losses as 11 Europeans killed and 11 captured, with a total of 200 askaris lost (Moyse-Bartlett (n.d.): 407). KARTUCOL's after-action report lists German European casualties as 15 killed, nine wounded captured and two unwounded captured (TNA WO 95/5328). A German history provides the combined casualties for 30/31 August and a 6 September encounter between the Schutztruppe and KARTUCOL as: among the Europeans, nine killed, 25 wounded, five missing; among the askaris, 30 killed, 108 wounded, 46 missing; among the African carriers, who also served

The new and the old used by the supply service: a carrier column passing a truck. Even for the British, the human carriers remained vital as a means of moving supplies forward. The British are estimated to have conscripted around 1 million African carriers from their colonies and German East Africa; of these, 95,000 died. The Germans did not keep records of carrier conscription and losses, but recent estimates are that as many as 350,000 carriers were employed. Without the carriers, both the Schutztruppe and the King's African Rifles would not have been able to prosecute the war. (© IWM Q 15418)

as a source of replacements for the Schutztruppe, 13 killed, 62 wounded, 242 missing (Boell 1951: 420). The differences in numbers for European casualties throughout the campaign may be due to the British counting all Europeans as Schutztruppe and the Germans excluding the 'non-combatant' Europeans of the civil service and medical personnel. One complete German field hospital was lost along with its valuable medical supplies, as well as a large portion of the Schutztruppe's store of rifle spare parts.

For KARTUCOL, the two days of fighting around Lioma was the best chance it had to inflict a decisive defeat upon the Schutztruppe. The causes for not doing so were many, and Giffard's after-action report provides the on-the-spot commander's view of why Lettow-Vorbeck escaped and survived. This report also provides a good summary of the difficulties of bush warfare:

(1) He was reported having gone South and though the position of his camp was known to 1/1st KAR it was not reported to me till too late for me to attack as the enemy had already left it before the report reached me.

(2) His attempt the night before to go NE led me to believe that he would certainly go NW in his break to the north as his Northeasterly and Northerly attempt had been frustrated. I had therefore moved 2/2nd KAR further west than I otherwise should have done and so left him a gap. Any attack I made therefore when he moved drove him in the direction he wished to go and 2/2nd KAR were too far away to be of use at the critical time.

(3) The whole of 3/2nd KAR was not put into the fight as the persistent reports from reliable officers to the South of enemy movements to the West compelled me to hold a reserve to cope with this movement and the movement was not reported as ceasing till 1130 hours when the enemy had succeeded in getting his stuff past to eastward.

(4) The difficulty which is always the same in the Bush of getting information accurately and quickly. (TNA WO 95/5328)

Not mentioned by the British commander, but evident to all, was the hard fighting of the veteran Schutztruppe and their determination to survive. British casualties during the two days of fighting were incompletely reported: 1/1st KAR suffered four Europeans killed and six wounded and 28 askaris killed, 53 wounded and 15 missing; casualties suffered by the three battalions of 2nd King's African Rifles were not reported.

Analysis

Despite claims by some authors that Lettow-Vorbeck invented bush-war doctrine, or that the Schutztruppe invented it before 1914 and that the British were ignorant of bush warfare, pre-war British colonial officers had in fact studied and developed doctrine, tactics and techniques for bush warfare that were little different to those of the Schutztruppe. British officers were well acquainted with bush and jungle warfare in Africa, India and Burma, and frequently wrote about their experiences and lessons learned. An example is the book *Bush Warfare*, written by a Canadian-born graduate of the Royal Military College of Canada, William C.G. Heneker, and published in 1906. Heneker became a regular British officer in 1888 in 1st Battalion, The Connaught Rangers and later served extensively in West African bush campaigns. Descriptions of tactics, employment of machine guns and artillery, carrier columns, patrolling and other topics are found in this book that are applicable to describing operations of both the King's African Rifles and the Schutztruppe. The decision by veteran British generals in early 1917 to drop

Led by a European, Schutztruppe askaris march through the bush near Tanga in 1914. A common image of the East African campaign is that of a few Germans and a loyal band of askaris fighting the might of the British Empire and remaining undefeated until the end of the war. In reality, the isolated Schutztruppe was steadily ground down during the war by its opponent. This grinding process escalated as new King's African Rifles battalions became combat veterans and began to match the Schutztruppe in bush-warfare skills, many of which were the traditional strengths of the East African fighting man and hunter. For the last year of the war, the Schutztruppe was a raiding force numbering fewer than 2,000 men reduced to living off the land and by whatever they could capture. (Photo by ullstein bild/ullstein bild via Getty Images)

Brig-Gen O'Grady reviews a King's African Rifles battalion on 4 July 1917, before the start of Linforce's main offensive. Soon, this unit and its brethren would prove their mettle against the Schutztruppe. O'Grady was highly regarded by the rank and file of the King's African Rifles for his bearing and the courage he displayed in combat in the bush. The troops and their Vickers machine guns are in formation on cleared ground with the European officers in front of their commands. The remnants of larger bush plants can be seen, giving one a sense of the size of East African bushes. (© IWM Q 46409)

the brigade-and-division structure in favour of a system of flexibly sized columns based on mission and carrier capacity directly echoed Heneker's suggestions on bush-war column sizes and their employment. Heneker also attempted to address bush warfare between modern opponents, i.e. European-type nations; the only historical case available to study at the time was the Spanish–American War of 1898. All that was missing from Heneker's *Bush Warfare* to describe operations in the East African campaign were Lewis guns, Stokes mortars, motor cars, aircraft and radios.

The Schutztruppe expanded immediately upon the outbreak of war, giving it a great advantage over the slowly expanded King's African Rifles. Lettow-Vorbeck ensured that all companies had European officer and NCO cadres by using colonial European settlers and stranded seamen in both command and technical roles. Initially, this resulted in Europeans manning, or at least leading and directing, Schutztruppe machine-gun teams. Because the period from August 1914 to March 1916 involved limited action, the new Schutztruppe companies could train, acclimate and establish a strong *esprit de corps* that served them well during the rest of the war. Cut off from Germany by the Royal Navy's blockade, with the exception of two blockade-runners, the Schutztruppe was forced to use what it had on hand in German East Africa or could capture.

As the war continued and the Germans retreated before the British offensives in 1916 and 1917, the limited supply capability they had built up in German East Africa was lost. Because the pre-war high wages paid to the Schutztruppe askaris were no longer on offer, the askaris had to accept the idea that they would be paid after the war – assuming there had been a German victory. Also, home areas from which askaris were recruited fell to the British and Belgians; some Europeans' and askaris' morale suffered as the territory they held gradually diminished. Desertion among askaris increased as some tried to return to their homes, while others (along with some Europeans) decided that capture was a better alternative. During the war, however, it appeared that as the numerical strength of the Schutztruppe declined, the morale and fighting spirit of the remaining force remained unshaken; the stout-hearted had remained with Lettow-Vorbeck and continued to follow him to the end. Because of their abilities to live and move in the bush and given their considerable combat experience, the surviving Schutztruppen were a match for larger but less-experienced British forces in the harsh conditions of bush warfare. The result was that smaller Schutztruppe forces were able to hold positions against superior British numbers and firepower and launch ferocious counter-attacks that frequently forced the British into a defensive posture; the Schutztruppe would then slip away to fight another day.

The performance of the Schutztruppe fighting against the Indian Army and European South Africans of Smuts' 1916 offensive came as a shock to most, but not to the veteran King's African Rifles officers. Soon, the British command, including South African generals, were clamouring for additional King's African Rifles battalions. A year and a half had passed, and the subsequent rushed expansion of the King's African Rifles cost many lives, both European and African, that an earlier expansion, such as that of the Schutztruppe, could have prevented. Recruitment yielded thousands of new askaris and enabled the formation of new battalions. At first, the British limited the number of King's African Rifles European component officers – in July 1916 there were 243 European and ten European NCOs – but in the second half of 1916 new King's African Rifles battalions began to reach the front. These units were composed primarily of new recruits and contained many European officers who lacked prior experience commanding Africans or of bush warfare. The first encounters between these new King's African Rifles units and veteran Schutztruppe companies resulted in frequent King's African Rifles defeats. As shown time after time in history, new formations going into battle against hardened veterans frequently suffer defeat. This in itself does not prove one side or the other is better; only periods of long, hard and realistic training can make a green unit perform well against a veteran one, and even then numerical superiority is frequently required. What these initial clashes did was to provide the toughest training school possible for the new King's African Rifles battalions. After each fight, the survivors, European and African, learned what worked and what did not; and having come through the experience of actual bush fighting, they began to understand what to expect the next time they met. As 1917 progressed, the King's African Rifles battalions were tempered and developed a cadre of experienced officers and other ranks that became the core of these units. In mid-1917 the British started incorporating significant numbers of European NCOs into the King's African Rifles: in July 1917, the European to African ratio was one to 35; in July 1918 it was one to 11½. The increased number of Europeans coincided with the increasing experience of the King's African Rifles battalions, but it is not possible a century later to determine which factor played the greater role in the improved battlefield performance of King's African Rifles units. By this time, replacements joining battalions in the field were living side by side with veterans who taught the newcomers how to survive and fight in the bush.

By August 1917, several King's African Rifles battalions, such as 1/2nd KAR, could hold their own against the best of the Schutztruppe. Even so, the chaos of bush warfare could result in veteran units suffering defeat. In the summer of 1918, the veteran 3/3rd KAR suffered crippling losses during a confused firefight in Portuguese East Africa. Believing they had just forced a Schutztruppe detachment to withdraw from their front, they were busy setting up camp for the night when they were suddenly attacked from one side by Lettow-Vorbeck's main body and overwhelmed. The battalion had no idea that this enemy force was nearby; its scouts and patrols had not encountered it. The Germans were equally surprised to encounter 3/3rd KAR; it was simple luck that brought their column's line of march onto 3/3rd KAR's position unannounced, and the quick thinking of their advance guard led to the attack.

Schutztruppe askaris man a trench. The battles in East Africa qualify as minor skirmishes when compared to those on other fronts of World War I, and reports of 'heavy fighting' for the East African engagements may seem exaggerated. At the encounter at Narunyu the equivalent of 1½ British battalions, representing the main British effort that day, fought a 10–12-hour firefight against a German force roughly equal in size. The British casualties suffered on that day in East Africa amounted to a combined total of 41 dead and 145 wounded. In contrast, during an attack on German positions at Guillemont on the Somme front on 30–31 July 1916, one British battalion – 2nd Battalion, The Royal Scots Fusiliers – suffered 204 dead and over 300 wounded. The Scots were part of 90th Infantry Brigade, which suffered no fewer than 1,463 casualties. (© BArch, Bild 105-DOA7093 / Walther Dobbertin)

The operations of late 1917 and 1918 show both the Schutztruppe and the King's African Rifles moving and fighting as battle-hardened bush-warfare armies; and the performance of the King's African Rifles did not go unnoticed by the British leadership in London. The Chief of the Imperial General Staff, General Sir William Robertson, questioned van Deventer in October 1917 concerning the ability of King's African Rifles battalions to serve in other theatres. After several months of discussion the decision was made that once the situation in East Africa permitted it, a King's African Rifles overseas contingent would be formed. This would consist of two brigades, each of four battalions and one machine-gun company. The battalions would be the first and second battalions of the 1st, 2nd, 3rd and 4th King's African Rifles; the intended theatre for this force was Palestine. London's opinion of the King's African Rifles had come a long way from the War Office's dismissal of the force in early 1915.

The 'accountant's mind' may be inclined to regard Narunyu and other actions like it as mere skirmishes, or just the usual 'wastage' of personnel in wartime; but for a soldier under rifle and machine-gun fire, any fighting may seem heavy and frightening. To be killed or wounded is the same, whether it happens in a 'Big Push', a trench raid or a small firefight. One should not dismiss the reports of heavy fighting and heavy losses out of hand just because the 'butcher's bill' is not large; for in a battalion of 600–700 souls, a day's loss of 12 dead and 47 wounded, as with 1/2nd KAR at Narunyu, represents close to 10 per cent casualties. Many members of that battalion would probably have known one or more of the casualties. To these men, the day's work was heavy, and a friend or acquaintance would no longer be in the mess at dinner or around the campfire to share a joke. No matter how large or small a battle or firefight is, war is always hell to the fighting soldier. Both the Schutztruppe and the King's African Rifles askaris endured their own personal hells in East Africa and behaved as soldiers – but they were soldiers who were under-appreciated by the European nations they fought for.

Aftermath

Following the fighting at Lioma and the Pere Hills in late August and early September 1918, Lettow-Vorbeck led his remaining force into the south-west corner of German East Africa; and in late October the force was approaching the border with the British colony of Northern Rhodesia. Once more the Schutztruppe was pruned of the seriously sick and wounded; these personnel were left behind under command of Wahle, who was suffering from a hernia and required surgery that was beyond the capability of the surviving field hospitals to perform. Lettow-Vorbeck then led the force on an invasion of Northern Rhodesia. Time was running out for the Schutztruppe, however.

Once the war was over and the Schutztruppe had surrendered, the British treated the German white officers and NCOs almost as guests in East Africa. Here, Lettow-Vorbeck, seated in the chair, is surrounded by many of his subordinates in a group portrait. Because the Schutztruppe was the last German fighting force to surrender, many Germans felt that it did so undefeated. The British 1917 dry-season offensive, however, with a force predominantly composed of East and West African infantry, had reduced the Schutztruppe to less than a quarter of its April 1917 strength and forced the survivors to become a raiding force to survive. (© BArch, Bild 137-041595 / Foto: o Ang. I 1918)

King's African Rifles askaris in Burma. This picture shows askaris from Nyasaland (the old recruiting ground of 1st KAR and 2nd KAR in 1916–18) displaying a captured Japanese flag. Comprised mostly of King's African Rifles battalions, the 11th (East African) Division fought through the monsoon season during Fourteenth Army's offensive that defeated the Japanese Army in Burma. As in 1917–18, the King's African Rifles proved to be masters of bush and jungle warfare. (© IWM K 8631)

On 13 November 1918, documents carried by a captured British motorcyclist were brought to Lettow-Vorbeck: these informed him that an armistice had been signed ending hostilities and the war was over. On Sunday 25 November, at the town of Abercorn in Northern Rhodesia, the remaining 155 Germans and 1,156 askaris surrendered to the British. Lettow-Vorbeck and his Imperial German Schutztruppe passed into history, legend and myth.

By the end of the war, the King's African Rifles had been transformed from an internal-security constabulary of 21 weak companies into a modern infantry force of 18 field and four training battalions. Peace quickly brought reductions to the King's African Rifles: the 1 April 1919 establishment was six battalions numbered consecutively 1st to 6th, the wartime regiments each having been consolidated into single battalions. As events lurched towards World War II, however, Britain planned to expand the King's African Rifles in the event of conflict. In October 1936 the new Inspector-General of African Colonial Forces was Maj-Gen George C. Giffard, who had commanded KARTUCOL in 1918 and now prepared plans for an effective expansion of the King's African Rifles. As a result, the regiment formed its first new battalion in 1939, five more in 1940 and a further 11 in 1941. King's African Rifles battalions were critical to the defence of Kenya and the British offensive against the Italians in Somaliland and Ethiopia. A total of 37 new King's African Rifles battalions, including two machine-gun battalions and one battalion converted to a reconnaissance regiment, were formed. With six pre-war battalions this gave the regiment no fewer than 43 battalions during World War II.

In November 1918, the King's African Rifles, with its organization, weapons and tactics, was fully capable of bush warfare on an early-20th-century battlefield. But for the addition of radios, air support and armour, the King's African Rifles of 1918 was little different from British forces fighting in Burma where King's African Rifles veteran General Sir George Giffard commanded 11th Army Group during 1943–44. Knowing the quality of the regiment, Giffard requested it for service in Burma. Fourteen King's African Rifles battalions fought in Burma in the 11th (East Africa) Division and the separate 22nd and 28th (East Africa) brigade groups. The King's African Rifles passed into history when Britain's East African colonies became independent in the 1960s. The regiment's battalions were assigned to the new countries that contained the areas from which they were recruited, and most regimental traditions were soon forgotten or ignored as an unwanted legacy of colonialism.

UNIT ORGANIZATIONS

King's African Rifles rifle company

During 1916 a rifle company of the King's African Rifles was organized on paper to consist of six officers and 221 other ranks. After a short time in the field, a company could number between 100 and 150 men. There were four platoons, each of four sections of 12 men. In 1918 the platoon theoretically included a European platoon leader and one or two European senior NCOs. This number of Europeans was generally not achieved in the field. Companies did not have organic machine guns; these were organized at the battalion level into a half-company equipped with eight Vickers machine guns. When needed, battalion-level Vickers machine guns were attached to a company. Lewis guns were first allocated as two per company, but were soon increased to one per platoon, and these became central to small-unit tactics.

Schutztruppe *Feldkompagnie*

The *Feldkompagnie* was a unique organization with no parallel in the Imperial German Army. It contained three combat platoons numbering 60 men each. The *Feldkompagnie* included an organic machine-gun section, usually equipped with two machine guns, and a small signal section. The paper strength was 16 to 20 European officers and senior NCOs (including medical and non-combatant personnel), two African officers and up to 200 askaris. This official establishment was not changed during the war. By 1917–18, however, company strengths were as low as 100 men. Each company still manned two to three machine guns.

A road built in the bush to supply the King's African Rifles columns. During the 1917–18 operations, King's African Rifles units spent more time assisting with road construction – in 1918 the British built over 3,500 miles of roads, mostly in Portuguese East Africa – than in contact with the Schutztruppe. Today, many of the roads one finds on maps of southern Tanzania (formerly German East Africa) and northern Mozambique (formerly Portuguese East Africa) follow the routes originally built to supply the King's African Rifles and other British troops. (© IWM Q 15627)

ORDERS OF BATTLE

Narunyu, 18 August 1917

Linforce

Flanking column: 1/2nd KAR; 25th Royal Fusiliers
Demonstration force: 3/4th KAR
Reserve: 3/2nd KAR; 8th South African Infantry (not
    engaged)

Schutztruppe

Abt Wahle: 9., 16., 19. and 20. FK; 4. SchK; 'Tanga', 'O' and
    'S' Kompagnien
Reinforcements: 3. and 11. FK

Nyangao/Mahiwa, 16–18 October 1917

Linforce

No. 3 Column: 1/ and 3/2nd KAR; Bharatpur Imperial
    Service Half-Battalion
No. 4 Column: 3/4th KAR; 25th Royal Fusiliers; 30th
    Punjabis
Reserve: 3rd Nigerians; 8th South African Infantry (not
    engaged)

Schutztruppe

Abt Wahle: 3., 9., 19. and 20. FK; 14. RK; 4. SchK; 'Tanga',
    'O' and 'S' Kompagnien
Abt Göring: 4. FK and 8. SchK
Abt Kohl: 18. FK and 6. SchK
Abt Ruckeschell: 10., 13. and 21. FK
Abt Kraut: 2. and 25. FK
Directly under Lettow-Vorbeck: 14. and 17. FK; 3. SchK

Lioma, 30–31 August 1918

British forces

Lioma garrison: 1/1st KAR
KAR Second Column (KARTUCOL): 1/, 2/ and 3/2nd KAR

Schutztruppe

Abt Göring: 2. FK and either 3. or 13. FK; 3. SchK
Abt Müller: 9. FK and either 3. or 13. FK; 4. SchK
Abt Poppe: 11. FK; 6. SchK
Abt Stemmermann: 10 and 14. FK
Main body/baggage escort: 4., 17. and 21. FK

A British Voisin two-seater biplane at an airfield near Lindi in
November 1917. During the war, aircraft became a common sight to
King's African Rifles askaris as they flew reconnaissance, bombing
and liaison sorties. The surrender of the Schutztruppe's Westtruppen
in November 1917 is in part attributed to one British aircraft
dumping its bomb load to lessen its weight. The resulting explosions
convinced the Westtruppen's commander, Hauptmann Theodor Tafel,
that he was trapped; and with British forces to his rear and to his
front, he duly surrendered. (© IWM Q 15507)

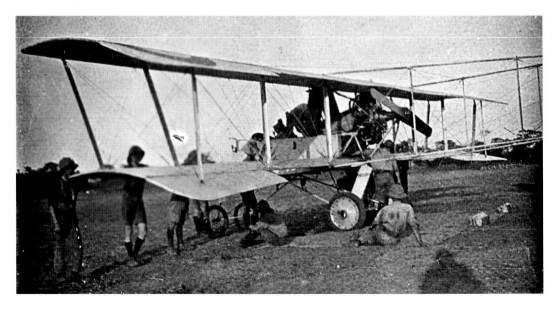

BIBLIOGRAPHY

Abbott, Peter (2002). *Armies in East Africa 1914–18*. Oxford: Osprey Publishing.

Anderson, Ross (2001). *World War I in East Africa*. PhD thesis, University of Glasgow. Available online at http://theses.gla.ac.uk/5195/ (accessed 11 February 2016).

Anderson, Ross (2004). *The Forgotten Front*. Stroud: Tempus Publishing.

Boell, Ludwig, (1951). *Die Operationen in Ostafrika*. Hamburg: Walter Dachert.

Buchanan, Capt Angus (n.d.). *Three Years of War in East Africa*. Uckfield: Naval and Military Press Ltd. (Originally published 1920, London: John Murray.)

Bull, Stephen (2014). *British Infantryman vs German Infantryman: Somme 1916*. Oxford: Osprey Publishing.

Downes, Capt W.D. (1919). *With the Nigerians in German East Africa*. London: Methuen.

Fecitt, Harry (2011). 'Lioma, 30–31 August 1918, The Final Great War Battle for the 1st Battalion of the 1st Regiment of the King's African Rifles', in *The Society of Malawi Journal*, Vol. 64, No. 2: 30–35.

Holdern, Lt-Col Charles (1990). *Official History of the War, Military Operations: East Africa Vol. 1*. Nashville, TN: The Battery Press. (Originally published 1941, London: HMSO.)

Lettow-Vorbeck, General Paul von (n.d.). *My Reminiscences of East Africa*. Nashville, TN: The Battery Press. (Originally published 1920, London: Hurst and Blackett.)

MacDonell, Bror (2013). *Mzee Ali: The biography of an African slave-raider turned askaris and scout*. Pinetown: 30 Degree South Publishing.

Miller, Charles (1974). *Battle for the Bundu*. New York, NY: Macmillan.

Moyse-Bartlett, Lt-Col H. (n.d.). *The King's African Rifles: A Study in the Military History of East and Central Africa, 1890–1945*. Uckfield: Naval and Military Press. (Originally published 1956, Aldershot: Gale and Polden.)

Nigmann, Col Ernst (2005). *History of the Imperial Protectorate Force 1889–1911*. Nashville, TN: The Battery Press.

Orr, Col G.M. (1924). 'From Rumbo to the Rovuma', in *Army Quarterly*, Vol. VII: 109–29.

Paice, Edward (2007). *Tip and Run*. London: Weidenfeld & Nicolson.

Samson, Ann (2013). *World War I in Africa*. New York, NY: I.B. Tauris and Co. Ltd.

Sheppard, Gen S.H. (1919). 'Some Notes on Tactics in the East African Campaign', in *Journal of the United Services Institution of India*, Vol. XLVIII: 138–57.

Sibley, Maj J.R. (1971). *Tanganyikian Guerrilla*. New York, NY: Ballantine.

Van Deventer, Lt-Gen Sir J.L. (1918a). Despatch, *Supplement to the London Gazette*, 5 April 1918.

Van Deventer, Lt-Gen Sir J.L. (1918b). Despatch, *Supplement to the London Gazette*, 16 December 1918.

Wienholt, Arnold (1922). *The Story of a Lion Hunt*. London: Melrose.

The National Archives (UK)

CAB 44/9: Draft Chapter XVII for unpublished *Military Operations, East Africa Vol. 2*.

CAB 44/10: Draft Chapter XVIII for unpublished *Military Operations, East Africa Vol. 2*.

WO 95/5328: 2nd KAR Column (KARTUCOL) War Diary, July–November 1918.

WO 106/273: Record of the 3rd Bn: K. A. R., during the Great Campaign in East Africa 1914–1918.

WO 161/75: 1st Battalion, 2nd Regiment KAR War History.

INDEX